SKIING WITH DEMONS II

THE AGENTS OF ENTROPY

SKIING WITH DEMONS II

THE AGENTS OF ENTROPY

CHRIS TOMLINSON

www.skiingwithdemons.com

YOUCAXTON PUBLICATIONS
OXFORD & SHREWSBURY

Disclaimer

Everything in this book is fictitious. The people mentioned never existed and the events described did not unfold. However, if everything in this book is a lie, which includes this disclaimer, then everything must be true! But, before this book disappears in a puff of logic, please read on - if its content entertains you, does it matter whether you think it's true or not?

Copyright © Chris Tomlinson 2016

The Author asserts the moral right to
be identified as the author of this work.

Cover illustration by Daniel House

ISBN 978-191117-547-6
Printed and bound in Great Britain.
Published by YouCaxton Publications 2016

All rights reserved. No part of this publication may be reproduced, stored in a retrieval system, or transmitted in any form or by any means, electronic, mechanical, photocopying, recording or otherwise, without the prior permission of the publisher.

This book is sold subject to the condition that it shall not, by way of trade or otherwise, be lent, resold, hired out or otherwise circulated without the publisher's prior consent in any form of binding or cover other than that in which it is published and without a similar condition including this condition being imposed on the subsequent purchaser.

YouCaxton Publications
enquiries@youcaxton.co.uk

Contents

Author's Notes	ix
1. The Ardent Incident	1
2. A First-World Problem	9
3. The Jamaican James Bond	14
4. A Skier's Guide to Existentialism	18
5. Skiing with David Icke	22
6. The Witness-Protection Programme	31
7. Going Off-Piste	34
8. How to Speak Franglais	42
9. In Search of Views	49
10. Trigger's Broom	55
11. The Agents of Entropy	64
12. Ski Like Nobody is Watching	68
13. Angry Pirates	76
14. Piste B - Marker 7	86
15. While You Were Sleeping	96
16. The Saga Louts	103
17. Failed Domestic Goddess	110
18. Powder Demons	116
19. The Soggy Bottom Boys	121
20. The Book Run	131
21. Boyfriend Skiing	137
22. Chalet Raspberry & The Cresta Run	143
23. Le Chat Noir	151
24. One Flew Over Laax	158
25. Women Behaving Badly	173
26. A Bad Bout of Entropy	181
27. The French Door Test	190
28. The Best Ski Instructor in the World	196
29. The Existential Party	203
30. Keep on Running	207
31. Vallée de la Manche	212
32. Midlife Clarity	219

Dedication

Debbie: thank you for your patience, tolerance and love.

'A man seldom feels like laughing on his own.'

Jean-Paul Sartre

Credits

I am also grateful to Jon Derry, Carol Hardcastle and Bob Fowke (the editor), who played their part in translating the original manuscript into English.

Author's Notes

People didn't recognise me - I could barely recognise myself. If that was the point of a midlife crisis, then mine had been successful. I was everything I used not to be and hopefully not everything I once was.

I was fit and sober (mostly), a ski instructor (theoretically[1]), a cook (passably), an author (finally) and, in the winter at least, I was living my dream.

In the summer I was a househusband and stepfather (inaccurately). I had a wonderful fiancée (genuinely), a fat Labrador (entertainingly) and lived in a large house in suburbia (unexpectedly). In the summer, I was living what I'd previously considered to be a nightmare, but it wasn't so bad after all.

I was divorced and heading for a second marriage. I'd taken a little equity and hopefully wisdom from my first, but my remaining chattels were stored in a garage in Sutton Coldfield - a town from which I seemingly couldn't escape.

I spent my winters living in a different garage, in Morzine, a ski resort in the French Alps. I worked there as a cleaner, a driver, a cook and a ski host. It was a job I'd created for myself as part of the Chalet Project – as my cunning plan to escape the rat race was called.

I'd written a book about the first four years of the project called *Skiing with Demons (SWD-I)* - a cathartic snowy self-indulgence that had been cheaper than therapy and happily had made me a few quid. It also made some people brand me a sexist, a fascist, a jingoist, an ageist, a narcissist and an alcoholic – and I was probably

---

[1] I passed my British Association of Snow Sport Instructors (BASI) Alpine level-1. Which, according to an actual ski instructor (a BASI- level 4) is the skiing equivalent of getting your 100-metres swimming badge.

guilty on all counts as charged. But unbeknown to me, I was really an existentialist waiting to be born.

This book is mostly a chronological sequel, although it includes my early encounters with snow and skis. Either writing is addictive or I simply needed some more therapy. Two years and, more importantly, two seasons have passed since the first narrative ended and readers may have assumed, the dream being actualised, that I lived happily ever after. But life is not like that – well, at least not mine.

I've also remembered, or been reminded of, some anecdotes that I regretted not including in the first book. It didn't really get finished to my satisfaction; it just got published instead. Some people were disappointed they hadn't been mentioned - well, fellow narcissist, you should be careful what you wish for.

This book describes more of the interesting guests I've had the pleasure to serve and the skiing professionals I've tried to learn from. It also contains more about the intermediate skiers who soldier on fighting their Ski Demons - despite being bruised, cold and frequently scared on their so-called holidays.

It also contains a lot of what I call 'chairlift philosophy', some of it sourced from those who dangle on worryingly thin cables with me, while breathing in very chilly air. It's mostly about surviving an existential crisis – and what that term actually means.

1. The Ardent Incident

It had been another long day in the office. The clients had treated me to lunch, a very important part of my working day - it was my only fee for being their guide. Now it was time to be their chauffeur and drive them back to the chalet.

It was January and Season 5 had just got into full swing thanks to a much-needed dump of snow. I was really enjoying being back at what I called 'work' after another long summer.

If I needed confirmation, and I often did, that I was 'living the dream' it was on my commute to work. After four consecutive ski seasons in the Alps I'd started to take many aspects of my winter life for granted and some had become mundane. However, the fabulous scenery still took my breath away and reminded me why I'd chosen this winter life.

Landie, my battered Defender, was the worst company car I'd ever had. In my previous life, the make, model and engine size of my car seemed important but, no matter how luxurious or fast my vehicle was, I'd spend more time in it screaming at the traffic, stressed about being late, than driving it on the open road. There wasn't a rush hour in this winter wonderland and the traffic was always light - I always enjoyed driving Landie on my commute to work.

Parking at the office was never an issue either. Landie could get to parts of the Ardent car park that lesser vehicles couldn't reach - I could always find a space right next to the piste. I used to brag that the chalet might not be ski-in/ski-out but the back of my Land Rover was.

I didn't always drive to Ardent. Not all my guests wanted a guided tour of the Portes du Soleil (PdS). If they did, the Ardent bubble provided direct access into Les Lindarets and beyond into Switzerland, avoiding the often congested Avoriaz area. So the twenty-minute drive there saved time.

The road from Ardent wound its way down to Morzine past Lac Montriond, a sight that could only be surpassed in beauty by its unfrozen self. I'd visited the lake during the summer too and seen the abundance of fish swimming in its turquoise water. Whenever I drove past in the winter I thought of them, now trapped in their ice-capped tomb, waiting for summer to return.

The lake usually has a square hole, made by ice divers, a hundred metres out from the bank. I always wondered what kind of lunatic wanted to go ice diving – perhaps lunatics who didn't find skiing exciting or dangerous enough?

I tried scuba diving once in Egypt and didn't really get on with it. The Ski Demons had obviously contacted their aquatic relatives (The Dive Demons) and they got inside my head. When diving, it's important not to panic and shoot to the surface - something I had an almost irresistible urge to do. I never went deep enough to risk getting the bends if I did. However, my instructor had explained the respiratory damage a rapid surfacing might cause – ironically, while she puffed on a fag. In the Red Sea, the reward for taking such risks are obvious - seeing a coral reef at first hand. The attractions of floating in the dark under a sheet of ice are not so obvious - although it does take away the danger of premature surfacing, I'll admit. Anyway, back to skiing.

Despite its beauty, Lac Montriond has had a macabre past. Recently, it's been the site of a murder and a suicide. A jealous husband, suspecting his wife of infidelity, cut her air pipe and then his own, while under the ice. When I heard the story, it confirmed that my assessment of an ice diver's mental health was accurate.

The Morzine-Ardent road has a reputation for being treacherous. Friend and ski-shop owner, Michel, had warned me about the road many times, but I had not heeded him. It didn't seem that bad to me and, anyway, I was driving up and down it in a vehicle perfectly designed for the task.

I'd had one minor scare a few seasons back when the road was covered in snow, while I was ferrying a group of heart surgeons to their hotel. I was giving them my tour guide spiel, pointing out the hole and telling them about the ice murder, when I noticed that my brakes weren't being especially effective. I kept schtum and hoped that the decision not to put snow chains on wouldn't result in a major setback for Birmingham's heart-transplantation service where most of them worked - luckily it didn't.

That January however, the road was dry and I had been skiing with my favourite group of property developers, along with their lawyer. They'd been supporters of the Chalet Project since its conception and had become friends. We'd had a great day skiing and an even better lunch. I didn't give them my tour guide spiel because they'd heard it many times before, along with my opinions on ice diving. I decided to put some music on and get the après ski mood going.

The road ahead had been cut into the side of the mountain. Like many alpine roads, sections of it had concrete canopies to shield it from avalanches but the last such structures were behind us. The steep mountainside was covered in snow that flanked the road on its left, effectively creating a wall of snow. A small drainage ditch ran along the bottom of the snow wall and a tree-filled gorge ran down the right side of the road, which might have warranted a safety barrier had this section of the road not been long, flat and straight.

I took one hand off the wheel to fiddle with the portable boom box dangling from Landie's mirror and tried to turn it on. While doing so I noticed in the mirror that Landie's rear wheels were no longer following her front ones, but trying to overtake them.

I wasn't alone in noticing this overtaking manoeuvre, judging by the communal intake of breath. I took my foot off the accelerator and steered left into the skid. This appeared to work, and the rear wheels fell back into line with the front, causing everyone to breathe out.

Luckily there was no oncoming traffic because we were now on the wrong side of the road, heading towards the snow wall and its ditch. So I pointed Landie towards the right side of the road, only to see the rear wheels swing out to the right – we all breathed in again. I steered into this skid too, successfully, realigning the wheels, and we all breathed out. But now, although we were on the *right* side of the road we were heading towards the gorge, a far more worrying destination than the ditch – once again we all simultaneously inhaled.

This time I dabbed the brakes while applying the opposite lock, but this seemed to increase the arc of the pendulum that the back of Landie had become. We headed back to the ditch, everyone exhaling. Nothing I tried seemed to dampen the pendulum's swing - I'd effectively become a passenger too. Each oscillation of the pendulum took us closer to the gorge or ditch in turn. It would swing back and forth several more times before our breathing exercises were over.

It was like watching the white ball bounce around a roulette wheel after putting all your money on black. The gorge was red and an encounter with its unyielding trees would mean almost certain death. The ditch represented black and an encounter with its snow wall would be far more survivable. Landie was the ball and she had an equal chance of coming to rest on either colour.

I've never been a gambling man. I've been to Vegas a couple of times, but the biggest risk I took there was getting married. Gambling is the *one* vice I don't have. This is because I've always considered myself to be an unlucky person - if such a person can exist. My pessimism has never really let me down so I only take risks if the odds are massively stacked in my favour. I always try and have a backup plan for when/if things go wrong because, being an unlucky person, they usually do.

I'd been taking a small, calculated risk every time I'd driven down that road, but now the odds had risen to fifty-fifty and there was no backup plan; it had turned into a gamble and we were all in.

Now that I was a passenger and a gambler, there seemed to be lots of time to reflect. Many say your whole life flashes before you when you face imminent death and that the slideshow takes only a few milliseconds to complete. Time definitely stood still for me and I remember some of my thoughts.

Three years earlier, at my lowest ebb, I wouldn't have been that bothered which colour the metaphorical ball landed on - except that red, in the short term at least, might be more painful. That wasn't something I generally shared with people back then. Nobody wants an apathetic fatalist with suicidal tendencies for their chalet host, let alone their driver. However, while watching the metaphor spin, I realised that things had significantly changed for me - I had quite a big stake on black.

Apart from the irritation of my own looming death, five other souls shared my fate and I really didn't want to be responsible for theirs. I consoled myself with the thought that at least they were property developers, not heart surgeons, and their death would be less of a loss to humanity - if more than my own.

I then noticed the lawyer was sitting next to me and he was wearing his seat belt - as unusually was I. We stood a much better chance of surviving a tumble down the gorge than those in the back who were not. Nobody wants to survive a fatal crash they might have caused and you certainly don't want the other survivor to be a lawyer.

Also, I regretted chucking the skis in the back with their owners instead of putting them on the roof rack. Should we roll down the gorge they would make effective blades in the human liquidiser the back of Landie would become.

Next I felt annoyed. If I died I wouldn't be able to finish my book. Would it get published posthumously? On the positive side, my death would probably help sales. Perhaps I might end up only badly injured? I was looking for a more dramatic last chapter - this could be it. The book would have a pleasing symmetry if it started and ended in a French hospital.

I had other unfinished business too. Not least the stew I had left in the slow cooker that morning. I was irritated that, having gone through a lot of trouble reshaping my life (and peeling the vegetables for the stew). I wouldn't have enough time to enjoy it. I'd previously professed to want my death to come through misadventure (in a none-alcohol related incident) but I'd envisaged it being a far more glamorous event and some distance in the future — although this was at least a beautiful spot to die.

If I did die or, worse, simply got injured, who would run the chalet? I'd let a lot of people down. I might not be too upset at dying, but it would really damage my business - my family (new and old) would be quite upset too.

After five swings of the pendulum, the front left wheel went over the edge of the ditch pulling Landie into the welcoming bosom of the snow wall and time returned to its normal pace. We ground to a halt, tipped up on our side at a forty-five-degree angle, with the left-hand wheels in the ditch and the front right-hand wheel in the air. I was the first to speak.

'Well, that was exciting. Everyone okay?' I enquired. There was no immediate reply, presumably my passengers were doing a self-assessment before speaking or were simply lost for words. I turned to see four ashen faces looking back at me. I don't remember exactly what was said next, I do recall a lot of expletives, but the general sentiment was along the lines of 'thank *fuck* for that' - never have six blokes ever been so glad to find themselves in a ditch together.

I climbed out of the elevated driver's door and the lawyer followed me - the snow bank prevented him from opening the passenger door. Mercifully he was uninjured. Those who had narrowly escaped liquidation spilled out of the rear door. Some crossed the road and peered down the gorge giggling nervously. I started assessing the damage to Landie, which was surprisingly light, and started chuckling to myself – perhaps I wasn't such an unlucky person after all?

Unfortunately, Landie's differential lock *was* broken and wouldn't engage, so I could only get power to the airborne wheel, which wasn't terribly useful. A snowplough went past, the driver more annoyed at the obstruction we were causing than interested in our plight, then a passing Land Cruiser did stop and the driver offered to pull Landie out. Despite the humiliation of having my nation's finest off-road vehicle rescued by Japan's, I accepted. Luckily I had a towrope, more commonly used by me to rescue other vehicles than to rescue myself.

The Ardent Incident, as it became known, shook me to the core. It wasn't the first or indeed the last time I'd be a passenger behind Landie's steering wheel, but nothing quite so dramatic had occurred before or has, thankfully, since. I turned into a nervous driver for most of that season and seldom drove to Ardent. Winning the gamble of my life had a more profound effect too – it sent me down a different philosophical road.

Having almost just lost my life, I began to wonder if I was wasting it. What exactly was the point of my existence? What purpose did it serve? Was I born to ski, eat and drink a lot, then die? How would I be remembered and what legacy would I leave? Was hedonism really for me? The ball landing on black had given me a second chance and I still had a useful amount of time left. Should I return to reality, get a proper job and start living a meaningful life? Was it time to end the Chalet Project? These questions preyed on my mind for most of that winter and the following summer too.

One good thing: the property developers obviously didn't find the experience particularly profound because they returned to Morzine and stayed with me the following year. They even rode in Landie – although they insisted the skis went on the roof and they did bring their lawyer again - but I made him sit in the back.

Each had a slightly different account of the incident and each account diverged further from the truth each time it was told - as no doubt does mine. I argued that black ice was the most likely culprit and my driving skills had actually saved their lives, not endangered them.[2]

My truth is that we were all both very unlucky and yet incredibly lucky at the same time that day – and, most importantly, we all lived to enjoy the stew.

---

[2] Some of the property developers were disappointed that the incident hadn't made it into my first book. But they should be pleased, like me, that it is now the first chapter of my second, rather than the last of my first - and indeed my epitaph.

2. A First-World Problem

During the winter I usually had little time for self-reflection. There were more practical problems to focus on: feeding my guests, keeping them safe on the mountain and keeping Landie on the road.

After four seasons of practise, I was consistently achieving these goals. I seldom gave anyone food poisoning, I regularly avoided death through misadventure and Landie made it back to the chalet most nights. I'd also achieved my humble skiing objectives: I owned an instructor's badge and a Ski Club of Great Britain jacket – neither of which I could wear outside in France. I was surplus to the Club's leading requirements that year. Thanks to their on-going dispute with the *École du Ski Français* (ESF) the Club had suspended its traditional leading service in France.[3] Just my luck, my blue leader's jacket was reduced to a trophy that I hung prominently on the back of the chalet door. Thanks to the ESF again, my badge could also only be worn inside.[4]

The thing I worried about most in the winter was how to survive the next summer. I really didn't have a long-term plan; I just existed without any purpose from May to November. This lack of strategy was starting to worry and occasionally irritate my saviour and main sponsor, Debbie.

---

3   The ESF have taken legal action against a Ski Club Leader for providing on-snow services without having the "proper" qualifications. The case is still on-going at the time of writing and no doubt at the time of reading too, given that the French legal system makes geology appear rapid.

4   The ESF only recognise BASI Level 4 instructors as qualified enough to teach on their slopes and will have anyone with a lesser British qualification arrested if they see, or think they are, teaching. At the time of writing, in all of the other Alpine countries, a BASI Level-2 qualification will suffice.

During Season 5, after the Ardent Incident, I reflected more on my long-term issues. How long could I live my new transitory life - indeed, how long did I want to?

The financial future troubled me too. I was no longer accumulating any wealth or contributing to a pension and I had no income protection or health insurance other than sleeping with a doctor (Debbie). I had no kids to look after me – although I know they don't come with guarantees. What would happen when I became too frail to be a chalet host - what would happen if I *didn't* die through misadventure?

After Season 5 was over, I returned to my man-cave in Sutton Coldfield to start my summer hibernation. I was worn out and glad to be returning to Debbie's house, a place that I was starting to call home. I would resume my role as her househusband. We were not married or even engaged at that stage, so 'husband' was a bit of a misdescription. I had problems sleeping in the summer, so 'hibernation' wasn't a particularly accurate description of my activity. If I did fall asleep I'd have some upsetting, alarming and often funny dreams.

Debbie was concerned about my summer insomnia even though I censored the contents of the dreams. She was an anaesthetist, not a psychiatrist, and offered more practical advice but I was one patient she couldn't put to sleep. I often reflected on that irony while lying awake next to her. It was rather amusing that an anaesthetist was sharing a bed with an insomniac, or it could have been. Despite it not being her medical speciality, Debbie diagnosed my psychiatric problem - I was having an existential crisis.

I wasn't entirely sure what that meant so I did what doctors hate most, I looked it up on the internet.[5] Sure enough I had the classic symptoms – people who search the web for ailments always do.

---

5   Thanks to the internet, we all self-diagnose, and it's the bane of a modern GP's life. Patients no longer just present with symptoms, they turn up with printouts too.

My life lacked meaning, purpose or value. I hadn't built an empire or amassed significant wealth; I hadn't discovered penicillin, or done anything to move humanity forward. I'd done nothing for the planet, except consume its resources. I hadn't even had kids to pass the existential baton on to.

I did feel one sense of achievement though: anyone can have a midlife crisis but I'd upgraded mine to an existential one. Only intelligent people can have them - or really rich ones. Not being the latter, I must therefore be the former, so I congratulated myself.

The good news was that my midlife crisis was officially over. You can only upgrade to an existential crisis when you've got the basics of life re-established: food, shelter, health, security and love. It's only after all that's sorted out, when you no longer have real practical problems or any physical pain, that you can make up some bogus problems to replace them.

The Ardent Incident had also made me reflect on my old life and the things I'd said and done. The way I'd been treated and had treated others was cause for a lot of regret. It was probably inducing the reoccurring nightmares, featuring people and arguments from the past.

When lucid, I always concluded that my new life was much better than my old one. It was a particularly easy life too in the summer. I was living over my place of work and sleeping with the boss. I did feel guilty about enjoying luxuries I hadn't earned, but I soon got over that. I told myself, I had first-world problems and I was unlikely to starve to death. I had a bright future and a comfortable retirement with Debbie lay ahead - if I didn't kill her kids before they left home.

Nothing can truly prepare you for becoming a step-parent - although being a chalet host comes quite close, especially if most of your guests have clearly never lived without domestic staff and don't think about leaving a tip. I'd been warned before I moved in with Debbie, that it wouldn't be easy. However, I'd had a stepfather, who had moved in when I was of a similar age to my new step-kids and it had worked out well. (Although, he might not remember the transition being so smooth - he's keeping schtum.) To start with, young children don't mind their parents being happy so long as it doesn't mean their stepparent is happy too. But, like most step-kids, I eventually understood that the annoying intruder made my real parent happy and that was almost as important as my own happiness. I'm now glad my mother found a second love and that she will not spend her retirement alone. Anyway, back to existentialism.

I'd left a few conflicts in Sutton the previous summer that were yet to be satisfactorily resolved. My solution was often to retreat to my man-cave and get on with the 'Bloody Book' (Debbie's working title for SWD-I). I frequently deserted my househusband post by going on lots of fell-walking trips - retreating to the mountains in the summer as well as in the winter.

The Doctor's advice was to get a proper job and do something useful with the rest of my life. I sensed a little understandable resentment that she was subsidising my summer life. She suspected that I lacked any ambition, which wasn't true; I wanted to be a writer and a geriatric ski bum. But I agreed, I did need a more realistic retirement plan.

Then the final nail was slammed into my existential coffin; Chalet Neige, my base in Morzine, was put up for sale. The owner was getting divorced – seems there's a lot of it about in the Alps. I couldn't afford to buy it nor secure a lease for the following season, so the Chalet Project looked dead in the water. The dream was over; it was time to wake up.

Without my winter life, my summer one didn't make any sense and I had no alternative but to rethink. There was no way out, I'd have to get a proper job.

However, in this new life of mine I was a four-year-old child. He had no marketable skills and, being stuck in the body of a fifty year old man, it would be hard for him to find employment. I know many middle-aged people, who have been made redundant, find it hard to find new jobs. I hadn't lost my job, I'd resigned from it, and hadn't been given a redundancy package. On top of that, divorce had halved my wealth. I could hear a chorus of friends singing, 'We told you so' - in fact that was one of my reoccurring dreams.

While searching for my symptoms online, I found the works of the French existentialists Sartre and Camus.[6] They, like me were a bit bemused about the purpose of life and how to correctly live – it was reassuring that I wasn't the first to agonise over these problems.[7] Reading, if not always understanding, French philosophy made me feel much better about skiing, eating and drinking to excess; I just had to find meaning in it. I had to somehow turn hedonism into existentialism – and that sounded much better than getting a job.

That summer, true to form, I decided to follow another foolish dream and try to become a professional writer. I started the Bloody Book II - and Debbie discharged her patient in despair.

---

6 **Camus** claimed he wasn't an existentialist and didn't know why his name was always associated with Sartre. Which is just the sort of thing an existentialist would complain about. They had a tempestuous friendship, which ended in a philosophical quarrel – unsurprisingly.

7 Sartre concluded that, 'Everything has been worked out, except how to live.'

3. The Jamaican James Bond

I first encountered snow when I was seven. The reason for the late introduction, despite being born in Yorkshire, was that I'd lived most of my short life in Jamaica – where it rarely snows.

My family moved to the Caribbean when I was three, my father having landed his dream job, working for the Jamaican government. I don't know whether to thank my parents for moving me, at the age of three, from Hull to paradise or accuse them of cruelty for returning me four years later.

It was snowing when we returned to England. I'd been told about snow and seen pictures of it but had no idea it was going to play such an important part in my life. It wasn't until I stepped off the train at Paragon Station in the centre of Hull, that I got some of it in my hands – and, to my astonishment, it was wet!

I remember scooping up my first snowball then licking it to see if it tasted like ice cream. It didn't, so I threw it at my sister. I also hadn't realised what a lethal projectile it would make, because her first encounter with snow made her cry.

Global warming hadn't been invented then and the UK still had proper winters. We'd returned to England in the depths of one of the worst on record. Hot-water bottles, wearing hats in bed and painfully cold toilet seats were all new experiences for me – we had no central heating. Once I'd got over the cold seats and the wetness of snow, I loved playing in the stuff: tobogganing, building igloos and snowmen and, of course, having snowball fights.

Post parental divorce, my mother, sister and I moved to a more rural setting and lived in my grandparents' house. They were living their retirement dream - a bungalow in South Cave. Well, they were until we moved in.

South Cave is now more of a commuter town for Hull than a country village. Its only claim to fame is that George Washington's great grandfather once lived there, although probably not in a bungalow. It also had a little-known outdoor ski slope called Mt Airey. It was more of a field on a hill with a footpath up it than a ski slope, but it was conveniently located behind my grandparents' house. It was on that hill, at the age of ten, that I first strapped on a pair of skis.

This was an age when kids had the right to roam on bicycles, and weren't ferried everywhere in 4x4s and generally kept in bubble wrap. At the weekends I was let out of the house with the cat after breakfast, free to wander as I pleased, neither of us expected to be back until we wanted feeding again.

That winter it had snowed heavily and my friend had found a pair of skis in his parents' garage, so one weekend we dumped our bikes and took them up Mt Airey. We hadn't realised that special boots were also needed to ski, so we used bailing twine to attach the skis to our wellingtons, with rather predictable results.

After that, my preferred vehicle for descending the Mt Airey slope was my much-envied toboggan. Most of my mates used fertiliser sacks – South Cave still had a farming community back then, before the 'offcomers' came and built their housing estates.

What my friend and I also didn't realise was that most people who could allegedly ski, wouldn't be able to cope with the conditions on the Mt Airey slope, even with proper boots. I had inadvertently tried skiing at its most difficult level (off-piste in deep powder), so no wonder I failed to master it.

There are many experienced skiers who never venture off-piste. Some of them, very sensibly, don't go out in bad weather either. I don't deride their lack of ambition, but I am envious of it. If you only ski one week a year and, after many years of pain, you're comfortably skiing on-piste maybe it's time to simply enjoy it – why press on with more torture? Then there are the masochists who can never reach that skiing equilibrium of enjoyment and pain. They see skiing as a sequence of escalating challenges - like a video game with levels of ascending difficulty. Once they become comfortable at one level, they want to move up to the next. Sooner or later they'll end up off-piste and some even end up dead.

While growing up, the only people I knew who went skiing were James Bond and the Royal Family. Well, I didn't actually *know* them - we moved in different circles. This was before the paparazzi had been invented and the only pictures we saw of the Royals on holiday were of them skiing in *Klosters* fully clothed. It seemed a rather glamorous and exciting thing to do and better than my annual family holiday - a camping trip to Wales.

After university, I mostly chose my own holidays and soon after I could finally afford to join Europe's elite and go skiing myself. My childhood conceptions of what a skiing holiday would be like hadn't matured. I'd also applied for a job at MI6 and assumed being able to ski was a prerequisite. So I went with my mates on an ill-fated and now well documented, trip to St Anton.

However, the pictures of the Royals and the Bond movies didn't give me any idea about how difficult skiing would be to learn or how much fear and pain would be involved. I hadn't really differentiated the skiing Bond did (mostly off-piste) from the skiing the Royals did (mostly on-piste) either. I hadn't appreciated that being able to ski wasn't a fixed objective and it had many levels of difficulty. Disappointingly, I didn't get the job at MI6 and ended up working in marketing.

In my thirties, I finally started to enjoy piste skiing and I told everyone that, along with the scenery, it was the act of skiing that attracted me. Having developed a political and social conscience, I generally kept the Royal Family out of it. I would explain that the mechanical aesthetics of skiing made my body and mind feel as one. Words I often remind myself of now when I'm in a whiteout, lost, cold and exhausted.

At the age of forty, rather than admit I still wanted to be James Bond, I told everyone that my desire to ski off-piste was all about accessing the mountains; I wanted to go places few people could, and experience nature at its wildest.

For most young men, who aren't so interested in scenery, wellbeing or the Royal Family, it's the adrenaline rush that attracts them to skiing: the speed and its associated danger. They also like the competitive elements of skiing - trying to go faster, further, higher, longer or steeper than their peers. Or maybe, they just like showing off to girls. If the latter is true they prefer the snow park where an audience can be found. If you see me in a half pipe – it's safe to assume I'm lost, not showing off.

There are no audiences when you ski off-piste. The only witnesses are the handful of people with you and they are hard to impress because they are often more accomplished skiers than yourself. I'm not an adrenaline junkie or especially competitive. I wasn't particularly looking for a new challenge. So I don't know why, after becoming a competent piste skier, I moved onto the next level – off-piste.

I did think that by sticking to the pistes I was cheating. I wasn't really moving at will through snow-covered mountains or going where I liked. I needed the snow to be pre-flattened to move anywhere on it. I wouldn't be a proper skier until I could ski on virgin snow and choose my own destinations.

The pistes were pre-prepared motorways and I wanted to go off-roading - or maybe I still wanted to return to Mt Airey someday, this time with proper boots, and pretend I was James Bond.

4. A Skier's Guide to Existentialism

The French have had many great philosophers and I'm not just talking about Eric Cantona.

First there was Descartes who famously said, 'I think, therefore I am'. Then came Monsieur Voltaire who thought, 'nothing can exist without cause.' Next came the existentialists: Sartre, de Beauvoir, Camus and Merleau-Ponty to name just a few in a random order. They basically thought we were all born by chance, died by accident and just *existed,* with a few irritating complications, in-between.[8]

Søren Kierkegaard, a Danish philosopher, is thought to be the 'father of Existentialism' but back in the 19th century the term 'existentialism' hadn't really been invented. A few Germans and Russians then got in on the act. After the Second World War, when everyone was a bit pissed off with humanity and God, the French made existentialism their own. Sartre was their ringleader and generally thought to be the preeminent existentialist.

Existentialism emphasises the individuality of existence, freedom and choice. It is the view that humans define their own meaning in life and try to make rational decisions despite existing in an irrational universe. It focuses on the question of human existence and the feeling that there is no purpose or explanation at the core of existence. The only way to counter this nothingness (and hence to find meaning in life), is by embracing existence.

---

8 Sartre summed it up best, 'Every existing thing is born without reason, prolongs itself out of weakness, and dies by chance.' He wasn't, by all accounts, a very cheerful fellow.

4. A SKIER'S GUIDE TO EXISTENTIALISM

The French existential movement wasn't just about philosophy. It included theology, drama, art, literature and psychology and its protagonists didn't agree on much. It came in plenty of flavours, both with and without a transcendent super being called God on top.

From an existentialist's point of view, skiing is very similar to life – it's completely pointless. Both involve a lot of effort, pain and emotional turmoil and have the certainty of a final destination. In skiing's case, that destination is the après bar; in life it's the graveyard. Although, skiing may facilitate a more direct route to the latter, most of us usually make it to the former.

Although the French existentialists often contradicted each other, their central axioms were the same. So I have created a list of them and suggested how they might apply to skiing. Feel free to disagree – disagreement is an important part of the existential beast.

1. Humans have free will.
    - I chose to go skiing.
2. Our nature is chosen through life choices.
    - I choose to go boarding.
3. We're at our best when struggling against our nature.
    - When fighting the Ski Demons.
4. Decisions are not without stress and consequences.
    - I should have taken the blue.
5. There are things that are not rational.
    - Drinking Jägermeister with Red Bull.
6. Personal responsibility and discipline is crucial.
    - I must wear a helmet. I must get fit.
7. Traditional religious and secular rules are arbitrary.
    - There is no right way to ski.
8. Worldly desire is futile.
    - As long as I have enough money to go skiing.

They also agreed on what existentialism wasn't:

1. Seeking wealth or fame.
   - I want to own a chalet, and win a skiing gold medal.
2. Social values and structure control the individual.
   - I must ski like my instructor.
3. Accept what is.
   - Moguls skiing will never be enjoyable.
4. Science will make everything better.
   - I need some better skis.
5. People are basically good but ruined by society.
   - They push in at the front of lift queues.
6. Having an, 'It is not my fault' mentality.
   - They made me drink.

I've probably just butchered existentialism and its history, but hopefully you get the general idea. You can do your own research, come to Morzine, buy me a pint and we can have a philosophical debate or maybe just go skiing?

Sartre, when answering the question, 'what is the meaning of skiing?' said, 'the snowfield is like the body of a woman. I want to take possession of it. I want to dominate it. The snow melts by virtue of my pressure upon it and enables me to glide across its face.' Okay, he was a bit weird and probably a bit sexist, but it was 1943 - so let's ski swiftly on.

He continued by saying: 'I, the skier, am an agent, I have intentions, and therefore I represent consciousness. The mountain, on the other hand, is never anything but a mountain. Nothing but matter, unambiguous and undivided, incapable of conscious thought or intentionality. My problem is that I want to be a skier in the way that the mountain is a mountain.' Not the most helpful of skiing tips, I'll admit. It does underline why mountains, by contrast, make us feel alive.

Along with wanting to ski like a mountain, Sartre had lots of other problems. Like most philosophers, he was trying to answer the impossible questions. What is the meaning of life? Could he even prove his own existence? How could he validate his existence given the seeming pointlessness of life? He came up with the catch phase, 'existence precedes essence' – an observation on life as esoteric as the observations he made on skiing.

He meant (I think) that human beings, through their own consciousness, create their own values and determine a meaning to their own life. First of all, I existed, then I went skiing and through skiing I define myself. Or put another way - being a skier doesn't define me, I just use skiing to define myself.

Sartre concluded 'I am, therefore I think' was a better proof of existence than Descartes' catch phrase. Camus went slightly further, with 'I rebel, therefore I exist.' And not a lot of progress has been made since then.

In practical terms, an existential skier would not wear a T-shirt that said, 'I ski, therefore I am.' His would probably say, 'I am, therefore I ski.' I hope that makes sense – it probably makes none at all. Hopefully, I'll make more sense of existential philosophy and how it related to skiing, as this book unfolds – wish me luck.

5. Skiing with David Icke

Skiing is a bit like marmite; you either love it or you hate it. When people go skiing for the first time it can go either way. If they make some rapid progress they like it; if they don't, they become exhausted, demoralised and hate it. The weather is quite important too. Progress is more likely to happen on a nursery slope in the sunshine than on a red run in a whiteout - which is initially why I hated skiing.

I'd made the mistake of going to Geordie Ski School when I was in my twenties. This involved being pushed off the top of a mountain in St Anton to see if I was a natural *like* – I wasn't. My so-called friends from Newcastle completely misjudged my athleticism, resilience and ability to drink shots. They inadvertently gave birth to the Ski Demons and ultimately a book.

Once my mental wounds had healed, a decade or so after the physical wounds, I agreed to try again. Good friends Val and David, who affectionately became known as the Ski Nazis, persuaded me to try again.[9] Like marmite, it's usually very hard to convince failed skiers to try again, but somehow they succeeded with me.

With a greater understanding of a debutant's dilemmas, they carefully managed my rehabilitation. Most importantly they took me to a beginner-friendly place, *Le Tour*, at the top of the Chamonix valley. Progress was made and I discovered that skiing could actually be enjoyable, and my wife and I started going with them every year. Unwittingly, we had become members of Val and David's skiing tribe.

---

9 A **Ski Nazi** catches the first lift up every morning and the last one down every night, no matter what the conditions are like. They seldom stop for coffee or lunch and will normally eat porridge for breakfast - They usually have no known association with National Socialism.

Most of the tribe were ten or so years younger than our illustrious leaders. The less politically correct members referred to the tribe as the 'Ski Nazi Youth' and sometimes I could see why. However, being of Jewish origin, I thought that was a little inaccurate, if not offensive - so I preferred to call it 'The Ski Tribe.' It was actually a very secular organisation and included: snowboarders, snowbladers and anyone Val and David came across and liked.

Val would organise the annual ski trip and we would go wherever we were told, bowing to her superior knowledge of what made a great skiing holiday. Her ability to read between the lines of a ski holiday brochure is still unsurpassed.

Organising a group ski-trip is a thankless task. It takes a phenomenal amount of effort to get everybody in agreement on a country, a resort and accommodation type - never mind selecting the dates. It also requires a great amount of diplomacy and advanced linear programming skills. Skiers have strong opinions on what makes the perfect skiing holiday - and it's a bugger getting the money out of some of them.

Val's solution was to be dictatorial: 'David and I are skiing here on these dates, do you want to come?' This wasn't a problem for me. I really didn't care if the locals called their mulled wine, *vin chaud*, or *glühwein,* and when you're a beginner, one green run looks very much like another. I was just grateful to be invited and blameless if wrong choices were made. Some of the Tribe were less easy going but, interestingly, they never offered to organise a trip themselves.

David delegated such organisational matters to Val. He was in charge of all on-piste activities and was our mountain leader. Given that we all skied like sheep, he was more of a mountain shepherd than a guide.

That first week in *Le Tour*, we stayed in a charmingly old, but slightly dilapidated chalet in *Montroc*. Our host was 'Chalet Dave', a forty something divorcee. He had picked us up from Geneva in his battered Defender, which subsequently broke down on the way to the resort. It turned out he was our cook, our cleaner and our ski-host, not just our driver, for the week (that sounds familiar).

He'd recruited a girl to help him but she'd quit the previous week. It's not unusual for seasonaires to quit after a few weeks, once they discover what being a 'chalet girl' actually involves. Although in her case I suspect managerial incompetence might have been a bigger factor. Having seen his plight my wife helped him cook and I even washed up at one stage, but despite obvious exhaustion, his enthusiasm never waned and we enjoyed our stay. Little did I know that, some twenty years on, I would become 'Chalet Chris'.

Sadly, eight years later, in 1999, an avalanche demolished the chalet, along with a huge tranche of *Montroc* killing twelve people. The disaster was described as a 'once-in-a-150-year event'. The destroyed buildings were a long way from the slope that initially collapsed and far from any obvious risk. However, the type of snow involved allowed the avalanche to travel across a flat region, where it could reasonably have been expected to stop. As it travelled it picked up speed and more snow, and slammed into the village at 60mph. Harshly, the mayor was prosecuted for not protecting the village despite avalanche planning across France routinely ignoring events that occur less than once every hundred years. I have no idea if Chalet Dave survived. Hopefully he was under his Defender with a spanner, somewhere nearer Geneva, when the disaster happened.

The following season, the Tribe went to a more upmarket chalet in La Clusaz, a small picturesque resort not far from Morzine. This time Chalet Jerry was our host, a well-organised and well-to-do

5. SKIING WITH DAVID ICKE

proprietor. He even had a dedicated chalet chef to doing the cooking and a chalet girl for everything else – my first encounter with such species and they set the bar rather high for others and indeed for myself.

I remember that the chalet had a very well-appointed honesty bar – something I hadn't encountered before either. I initially thought it was a bit of a risky concept, given that most people, and especially the Tribe, found skiing very thirsty work. But soon realised that it was actually very profitable for Jeremy as most people, it turns out, are reassuringly honest.

He targeted his business at the corporate market or so he told us. What that actually meant, I didn't know, apart from it being expensive and we didn't have to help cook or wash up.

I have been on a few corporate skiing trips: twice to *Lech* and once to *Courchevel*. I went as the pretend partner of a female friend on all three trips – but I'll save telling you about my life as a male escort for another book. Other than not picking up the bill for anything, not doing much skiing and having to endure lengthy work-related dinner conversations, I'm not sure how corporate trips differ. In my case, I gained a fascinating insight into the global bitumen market despite not knowing what bitumen actually was, and I had to sleep on a settee. However, it did prove good training for my future life as a trophy husband.

Despite having a Toyota Land Cruiser, Chalet Jerry preferred to use his own Land Rover Defender for running normal guests around, despite the Cruiser allegedly being a better off-road vehicle. I guess the Defender was more fun and it was certainly more patriotic. He was very trusting with his Landie, letting us drive it to a remote restaurant on the staff's night off (an adventure best left undocumented for legal reasons). However, hacking around the Alps in a Defender became an integral part of my ideal skiing holiday.

After *La Clusaz*, the Tribe went to *La Plagne*, then *Megève*, then *Verbier*. Each year our skiing improved, some more than others. By this time, I was going on ancillary ski trips with splinter groups of the Tribe who wanted to experiment with different, less fascist, skiing ideologies. My wife, however, was happy with one ski-trip a year. I was more of a collector than her too; I wanted to collect a piste map from every resort in the world after having skied their signature runs.

Her skiing development fell behind mine. If you only play golf once a year, your handicap will not improve very rapidly; if you only ski once a year, progress is slow, if not stationary. You might progress from snowplough to parallel turns one year, usually on your last day, then the next year you're back to snowploughing. I always think that, if something's worth doing, it's worth doing a lot – but maybe that's just how I excuse my excesses.

Finally, one year the Tribe went to Morzine. We stayed in The Farm House, which had a laidback atmosphere, yet professionally run by 'Farmhouse Dorien'.[10] Val had finally found her perfect skiing accommodation and we stayed there several times. More of a hotel than a chalet, it has a large communal dining table for those all-important egalitarian encounters. It also has a bar with a barman to keep you honest. One of the bedrooms is a converted *mazot*, a type of shed traditionally used for keeping valuables in. Historically chalets used large open fires for cooking and heating, making them prone to fire. I can only imagine living in a place and

---

10 Officially known as *Le Mas de la Coutettaz*, the **Farm House** is the oldest building in Morzine, and dates back to the 1700s. One of the rooms was used as a prison during the war – however, modern inmates will find the decor and the catering have been improved.

a time when crime was so low that your valuables were safer in your shed than in your house. Most *mazots* have now been converted to accommodation and, sadly, valuables are now kept in safes.

Dorien was the first ski-host to lead me around the PdS and I remember that day skiing with him well. He was taking the Ski Nazis round The Circuit and they had deemed me a good enough skier (whatever that meant) to tag along.[11]

I remember him telling me he was going on holiday the following week. I assumed he would be sipping cocktails on a beach somewhere for a relaxing change - no, he was going to Chamonix to do some *ski-extreme*. Which is exactly the sort of thing 'Chalet Chris' says and pretends to do now. I also take guests around The Circuit at least once a week if I deem them 'good enough' skiers.

After that first trip to Morzine I'm sketchy about which resorts the Tribe visited and in which order. I recall going to St Foy, Bad Gastein, Flaine and Morzine several more times. We even went to St Anton, where I laid to bed some Geordie ghosts – but we mostly went to France.

It was always fun trying to work out the chronological order with other members of the Tribe. We would try to match up the resort, the chalet and the entertaining people we shared them with.

'Was it *Le Tour*, where we met those coked-up city types?'

'Do you remember that undertaker from Barrow-in-Furness? Wasn't that *La Plagne*?'

---

11 **The Circuit** is a circular journey around the Portes du Soleil on relatively unchallenging pistes. It takes between four to six hours, depending on how fast you ski. There are many different routes and shortcuts, and it can be done clockwise or anti-clockwise. Every ski-host has their own version of The Circuit that he thinks is the best - it's more of a concept than a defined route.

'Where was that hotel with the oligarch and his harems?' 'Oh, that was Courchevel.'

'Remember riding the *chariot-du-fromage* through the restaurant in *Vaujany*?'

I also have trouble remembering which skiing memory belongs to which resort. I can remember incidents and the terrain but not the names of the pistes or the resort.

'Do you remember accidentally skiing over that frozen lake? *Mayrhofen?*'

'Where was it we got so lost we ended up in someone's back garden?'

'Do you recall skiing down that road in *Verbier,* trying to thumb a lift?'

'Was it Les Arc, where we got stuck in that cable car – all desperate for the loo?'

'Do you remember having to cut Andy out of that safety net?'

'Was it *Megève* where Steve skied into the back of that cow?'

'Remember that time we skied with Hermann Maier? Well, we were on the same piste!'

My holiday photographs aren't much help either; they're usually of the same people wearing the same skiing outfits. They're mostly in exactly the same pose: holding up a beer in a generically themed alpine restaurant or on a piste with mountains in the background. After a few years, I stopped taking my camera skiing.

However, in 2004 David changed his turquoise skiing onesie for a red spider-Jacket and black salopettes. He wasn't, and still isn't, a dedicated follower of ski fashion, so this change of outfit caused a lot of confusion on the mountain. However, being a significantly historic event, it proved useful for dating photographs. The Tribe now use it to delimit, what we call, the 'David Icke Era' of our collective history.

David Ike was a sports broadcaster who went a bit left field. He developed a conspiracy theory that claimed many prominent figures belong to the Babylonian Brotherhood, a group of shape-shifting reptilian humanoids who were propelling humanity toward a global fascist state. I sometimes look at politicians and wonder if he was right. Famously (like our David) he only wore turquoise. His skiing ability and views on existentialism are unknown.

During the post David Icke Era, the Tribe visited many other places; *Vaujany, Alpe d'Huez, Samoëns, Kitzbuhel, Mayrhofen* and *Chamonix* itself amongst them. It wasn't exactly, '*Venimus vidimus vicimus,*' more like, '*Venimus, skiedimus, bibimus,*' - we came, we skied, we drank.

Vaujany was the scene of the worst cable-car accident in French history. Eight people died when a brand-new gondola detached from its wire during testing in 1989. This happened *before* my visit, unlike the *Montroc* avalanche, in case you were wondering if disaster always follows me. The locals used the mangled steel remains to sculpt a commemorative monument that visitors pass when entering the village. I found this a little macabre and psychologically unhelpful, not being the happiest of ski bunnies when riding in large cable cars. Anyway, I salute their commitment to recycling at least.

Members of the Tribe came and went, but a hardcore of skiing fanatics persisted. The ranks were often swelled by offspring and debutants (some never to return), and an entire skiing dynasty evolved. Then, in 2011, the Chalet Project was born and the Tribe entered the Morzine Era.

Once Val had stopped laughing and realised I was serious, she seemed a bit reluctant to book a week at Chalet Neige, despite me being desperate for her patronage. She couldn't have been worried about my domestic skills because she'd never seen them – at that time they didn't exist.

Eventually she gave me the benefit of the doubt, as did many of the Tribe. Their support was invaluable as indeed was their feedback, although I wished they hadn't been quite so honest at times – but that's what true friends are for.

If you're a skier, you probably have your own ski tribe, the guys and girls you go with every year. You probably have tribal leaders like David and Val, foolish enough to organise the trip. I've noticed that skiing friends tend to stick together even if they only see each other once a year. Perhaps that's the key to keeping all your friends – not to see them very often?

6. The Witness-Protection Programme

Five years had passed since the Chalet Project began. I'd spent three summers living in what I called the Sutton Coldfield Witness-Protection Programme, because it sometimes felt like I was hiding from the vindictive criminal that was my old-self. I was now legally divorced and contemplating getting married again; I needed to deviate from my usual life path - try, fail, try again, fail better – this time it had to be a success.

When you lose your home, you lose more than just a roof. Along with losing your ex, you lose a sanctuary and a safe place to dream. You lose a lot of memories too and you lose important artefacts from the history of your life. According to Sartre, 'You can't put your memories in your pocket, you have to have a house', and mine were stored in a garage. A home is where journeys start and where they're also supposed to end, but mine hadn't.

My plan initially looked like the work of a genius. Nobody would have suspected the 'child hater' would be hiding in suburbia, living with two kids and a dog. Unlike most programmes, where the witness is moved far away from their hometown, I was still living close to mine and foolishly I occasionally wandered the streets of Birmingham and kept getting recognised.

I hated going into town. Nearly every street corner, shop, restaurant or bar had a memory of my former life. It was hard not to look back to the days when I ran my own company in Birmingham and think of them as halcyon, even though they weren't. I always felt a slight feeling of alienation when catching up with old friends in city bars standing amongst the armies of professionals, drinking after work in their suits.

The handler in charge of my protection was Debbie or, at least, it seemed she was intent that I came to no further harm.

We were also protecting two other witnesses, from crimes not yet committed – her two sons. I would rather have had Debbie to myself but being a caring and selfless mother was part of her beauty.

A chairlift philosopher once told me that, 'It is better to love than to be loved.' If you love someone unconditionally you're blind to his or her faults and that's the love a mother has for her children – they can do no unforgivable wrong. If you don't have that type of love, their irritating habits, however minor, prey on your nerves. Being the object of such love can make the recipient very selfish. In order to feel less guilty, you occasionally want to put your partner's needs before your own. Often they won't let you do that and the debt of gratitude weighs heavy.

Sartre's view was slightly different, 'Generosity is nothing else than a craze to possess. All which I abandon, all which I give, I enjoy in a higher manner through the fact that I give it away. To give is to enjoy possessively the object which one gives.' I think he meant that it's always better to give than receive - and sometimes people are greedy and give too much.

Having a child might look like a one-way street, but it's the parent, by being allowed to give, that benefits the most - it is indeed better to love than be loved.

When you enter a protection programme they give you a new life, but most of it is spookily similar to your old one. You may shop in a different supermarket, but you buy the same things. You go to the same DIY store even though you're maintaining a different house. You load the dishwasher daily only it's a different make and you don't remember buying the cups and plates. The wardrobe is different but the clothes hanging inside are yours. It's a different TV but the programmes you watch and the series you follow are the same. Well almost – mercifully I no longer have to watch the X-Factor.

When you're on a Witness-Protection programme, no matter how well you commit to your new life, you feel like an actor playing a role and you feel slightly disconnected from the real world. And if you feel like this and you haven't recently moved homes - you too are having an existential crisis.

I kept in I touch with my old in-laws and occasionally met my ex-wife in town. We'd done and achieved many amazing things together – not least getting divorced without spilling too much blood on the streets. Friends had told me that only time would heal my wounds. And, although at the time I didn't want it to be true, they were right, it had. Three years on, there was little bitterness left, just shared memories and even though we were now sailing in different ships, it felt right to keep in radio contact. 'Freedom is what you do with what has been done to you' – you've guessed it, I'm quoting Sartre again.

For a protection programme to be effective, the subject needs to sever all links with their past – I hadn't. However, even if I had, humans are the sum of all they have said and done, and memories can never be erased. We're always in psychological danger from our past, no matter how far we run away.

Man was designed to have only one life and to complete it in fifty years, justifying his existence by having children and preferably with only one wife. Now, thanks to medical science, many of us have time to live twice. It's not always a good idea to separate those lives with a midlife crisis - it causes too much existential angst.

7. Going Off-Piste

Along with the other members of my Ski Tribe, I slowly mastered skiing's lower levels. After a few seasons, most of us could confidently ski down blues and reds and some of us found ways of consistently staying upright on black runs.

Seemingly unhappy with the amount of snow the Tribe were eating on an average day's skiing, David started to encourage us to venture beyond the piste marker poles. He would make little forays into the snow at the side of the pistes or cut from one piste to another hoping we wouldn't notice and follow him, then look very disappointed if we did notice and didn't follow.

However, crossing the pole line was like diving into an ocean for me. It literally meant holding my breath until I resurfaced back onto the piste. My skis didn't seem to work off-piste – well, not in the way I used them anyway. This wasn't just the next level; it was a completely new sport. I was back to being a beginner again and the marmite problem was starting to resurface. I wasn't fit enough to be a beginner and, after developing a reasonably good record for staying erect, I was out of practise at falling over - or rather, getting back up again.

I'm not sure why I kept following David. I wouldn't say I was a masochist and I thought I understood the concept of a holiday, of which the purpose is to relax and have fun.

David persisted with his off-piste forays, even though he lost most of his followers at the marker poles but a few of us who were more ideologically aligned kept following him. Confidence grew and he started to go further and further away from the piste, dragging us with him. The Ski Demons would always chirp up if I lost sight of the piste poles: would David get me into something I couldn't ski out of - a gully, a forest or a terrain trap that I wouldn't have enough energy to crawl out of? The problem wasn't my confidence in him, but his surprising confidence in me.

Those who followed David past the poles were having similar marmite problems. We developed an off-piste strategy called 'Turn, Recover, Celebrate' (TRC) - each successful turn off-piste being a triumph. We weren't really skiing the off-piste, just surviving it. We did occasionally link turns together, but they were more a sequence of linked recoveries, which warranted a larger celebration.

We had plenty of home-grown advice, but there was no actual professional instruction to be found, or so it seemed. Every time I booked an off-piste lesson, the instructor seemed to bang on about the usual body position and pole-planting stuff for making nice carved turns on a well-groomed blue. Nothing seemed to work as well as the TRC methodology that I was now the master of. The problem with skiing at any level is that, once you've found ways of staying erect, it's very hard to abandon them in order to improve.

I'd developed methods for dealing with most situations; little jump turns, sidestepping and side-slipping were all in my repertoire. I even developed something I called the Laydown Turn, which I think is self-explanatory.[12] But my nemesis wasn't the steeps but the deeps. The steep slopes didn't faze me, but deep powder did; if my skis were under the snow, the TRC methodology didn't work.

Each holiday, Val would hire a guide for a day to take her and David into the backcountry. Presumably because David was looking for his next level, or maybe he simply wanted a day off from leading the Tribe. Despite his next level being at least a couple above mine, he always encouraged me to go along. Knowing I'd end up being Tail End Charlie (T.E. Charlie) I usually refused.[13]

---

12 The **Laydown Turn** involves lying down, rolling over to point the skis in the other direction, and standing up again.

13 Being **T.E. Charlie** involves listening to well-meaning, yet condescending encouragement all day, while trying to keep up with faster skiers.

Then one year, in a place called St Foy, I agreed to go with the Ski Nazis on their annual backcountry trip. I knew another member of the Tribe was going and by my reckoning, she would struggle even more than me to keep up - so I would escape being T.E. Charlie. It's always good to take at least one patsy along to avoid being T.E. Charlie yourself. Now I come to think about it, this was probably David's reason for always inviting me.

Unbeknown to David, Val had hired a crazy guide called Bernard for the day. I know it's customary to precede the word 'guide' with 'crazy' but Bernard was clearly bonkers, you could see it in his eyes. He wanted to take us to the place of his youth, an abandoned village only accessible on skis in the winter and by goats in the summer.

He did the usual ESF guide's warm up: skiing a couple of reds to assess our ability by using the eyes in the back of his head. What relation our on-piste ability had to our off-piste ability, I didn't know. We all must have passed his test, because he unceremoniously turned off the piste and headed into the unknown.

The Unknown is one of the worst Ski Demons. Once you've lost sight of the piste markers, how long it will be before you return to their safety is unknown. Even if the guide has reassured you it will be easy, the difficulty of the terrain you'll encounter is still unknown because the guide's definition of 'easy' will not necessarily be the same as yours. Around every corner there's more unknown. There may be some obstacle that requires a tricky manoeuvre that you've not yet mastered. But overcome it you must – there's no going back in skiing; there's only forward and down.

We were soon out of sight of the poles. We traversed some distance round the top of the hill to a valley on its opposite side and there would have been no way for a tourist to know that the valley existed; it was completely hidden from the pistes. Bernard had already earned his fee.

The valley had a stream running along its bottom and a scattering of leafless saplings sticking out of the snow that looked like stubble on a giant's chin. I'd never seen an untracked, snow-covered valley before. Apart from needing a shave, it was pristine.

Not a single building, fence, domestic animal or human could be seen, the only tracks we could see were the ones we'd made ourselves. There was no evidence of humanity's existence at all - until an aeroplane ruined it by flying overhead.

We descended into the valley, in my case one turn at a time, then the patsy (she was actually called Debbie, albeit a different one) fell over, taking all the pressure off me, and I started to relax. At the bottom we crossed the stream using a snow bridge that nature had kindly provided. I decided to let Debs have a break and went last. But being the heaviest in the group, the bridge collapsed, leaving me knee-deep in a watery slush, much to everyone else's amusement.

Sometimes it's best to go first and sometimes it's best to go last. The trick is to know, in any given situation, which of the two applies. If you're committed to doing something scary, going first is better, rather than waiting and potentially psyching yourself out. In other situations it's better for someone else to discover the true perils that lie ahead. If it's not obvious, going somewhere in the middle is usually best. In the case of a snow bridge, first is most hazardous because you're determining if it will hold the weight of a human and it's also important to send the fattest bloke over first. But with every passage it might weaken so you don't want to be last either. By definition, the very last person to attempt the crossing will be the one that ends up in the drink. Ideologically speaking, you always want to be the second to last person ever to attempt a crossing of anything.

Those who had successfully crossed the bridge pulled me out and we continued our journey, in my case, with frozen feet. Despite my anxiety, the route to Bernard's ancestral home wasn't very difficult. We alternatively climbed up relatively gentle hills or skied down their backs in a foot or so of powder. None of the descents were really steep enough to require turns. It was a simple matter of putting your skis in Bernard's tracks and trying to shush up the next incline, before dismounting and walking to the top.

By lunchtime we'd made it to the village, a truly enchanting if eerie place. We sat outside one of the derelict buildings and admired the view, the sort of view I was after for my own fantasy home. I briefly wondered if I could live there permanently. The building would take quite a lot of fixing up but the neighbours wouldn't object. It wouldn't be possible, I concluded - it would be too difficult to get decent broadband.

Bernard presented me with some antifreeze for my feet. He pulled out a hip flask of homemade génépy and offered it round – and it worked. I enquired in to the recipe hoping it might be a family secret that he'd be prepared to share.

'*I go to zee bricolage* (DIY store) *and buy zee alcohol, I put in some génépy* (wormwood) flowers *and un peu de sucre* (a little sugar)', he explained. 'What's next in the process?' I enquired, expecting it needed some lengthy time to mature. '*We drink it of course!*' he replied, with a rather surprised face.

A little alcohol is a useful thing. Skiing is all about confidence and the best way to get down something is to mentally scream, 'attack, attack, attack', something alcohol helps with. Of course, too much alcohol and your ability to make correct decisions can be impaired. You'll know when this has happened if you find yourself skiing in a half-pipe, backwards down a red run or off-piste screaming 'attack, attack, attack' out loud. It's best to use alcohol in moderation – I'll let you know when I've worked out how.

Fuelled by génépy, we all skied much better that afternoon. Although, I did fall over several times, nothing insurmountable materialised. My first real backcountry experience had been carefully managed, maybe more by luck than judgement and on the whole I'd enjoyed it. It had really been a day of ski touring, without couloirs, crevasses and hidden cliffs to worry about.

There could have been avalanche danger, but at that time I was oblivious to such risks. I remember Bernard testing each slope before letting us descend it, by violently jumping up and down on the same spot. This, I subsequently discovered, is a common way for guides to assess the stability of the snow. I still think it's a bit like pulling the trigger of a gun to check if the safety catch is on.

Despite the frozen feet and the anxiety of the unknown, it had been a seminal day. I loved the tranquillity of the backcountry. I'd enjoyed meeting my first crazy guide, listening to his stories and drinking his skiing fuel. I'd enjoyed the camaraderie with my friends and I'd enjoyed the human-less valley.

Not all future backcountry trips were quite so enjoyable but I was now part of the Off-Piste Tribe. It was fun exaggerating to the rest of the Tribe about the extreme skiing we'd done, while they'd been pointlessly pootling around the pistes all day. There was always some event or incident we could laugh about, a spectacular wipe out, a tricky traverse, a couloir of certain death or emotional outburst. Going on backcountry trips made me feel and sound like an intrepid explorer, and it felt good.

Some of us are not happy sitting on a beach for the whole holiday and going home with a tan. No matter how luxurious, or opulent the surroundings, I usually get bored. There are those who seek action and those who seek relaxation and I want a balance of both. Sometimes it's not enough for me to look at a nice view; I feel the need to get in it, although not always up to my neck. Often the best holidays are not the most memorable ones. It's the ones that go wrong that usually end up in your memoirs.

One person's idea of a holiday is another one's idea of hell. I hate beach holidays; you spend all day sweating, worried about sunburn and dehydration, then in the evening you eat and drink to excess - oh, hang on a minute, that's skiing. Some people don't see being cold and wet, while having your feet tortured as much of a holiday either. However, if being comfortable and warm is the main requirement, why not stay at home and turn the heating up?

If relaxation is the primary objective, it may truly be better to say at home. The very act of going on holiday is stressful, unless you have your own private jet. Once you get to your preferred climate, you have to re-establish the basis of living, that presumably you've got sorted at home. Even simple tasks, such as turning on the shower, become problematic. You have to interact with strangers, often in a foreign language, every time you want food; at home you can simply open the fridge. You have to operate with a subset of your wardrobe and worry about everyone ripping you off. That's why when most people get back from holiday they say – 'ah, it's nice to be home.'

I got better at dealing with the unknown, and the more I skied off-piste in the PdS the more I knew what was around each corner. I always knew where the nearest piste was and therefore which direction to crawl, should I come to grief.

Even though, I'd conquered the steeps with the TRC methodology, the deeps still challenged me and if they had trees on them they were to be avoided - there were still many more skiing levels to master.

I'm not sure why I decided to take on the new sport of off-piste skiing. Did I simply want to get to the next level or visit hidden valleys to get more exclusive views? Or did I simply not want to disappoint David? Was I finally going to find my skiing equilibrium, somewhere beyond the piste marker-poles? Surely I didn't still want to be James Bond?

8. How to Speak Franglais

I hated being asked if I could speak French. It was embarrassing to admit that, after four winters in France, I hadn't got much past *bonjour*. But I had my excuses well practised.

At school, French was my *bête noire*. I was in the top sets for most subjects, but French was complete Greek to me. I could blame my teachers, but actually I soon gave up on what I thought was a lost cause. If I'd known I was going to spend so much time in France I might have tried harder. However, I was struggling with English at the time and learning another language seemed counterproductive (I'm still a long way from mastering English – as my proof readers will testify).

At that time, the problem for kids who were dyslexic, or 'not very good at spelling' as it used to be called, was that we had no earthly way of showing our intelligence. The arrival of the Rubik™ Cube eased matters, but it wasn't until computers were invented that we could really start to prove everyone wrong. Even though the geeks have now inherited the Earth, those with linguistic brains still take delight in correcting our spelling and implying we're thick. It's then hard for a mathematical brain to think of a good retort - it's difficult to form a suitably cutting retort just using numbers.

I used to answer the question in French, '*Je parle mal le français*' and hope the enquirer would think I was being modest and they would leave it at that, but often they didn't and a schoolboy French duel would ensue – which I would invariably lose.

I then started telling people that I spoke 'Eric Morecambe French' - I used all the right words, just not necessarily in the right order - which was partly true. I spoke Franglais - that idiomatic blend of French and English that is well practised by us Brits, yet little understood by the French.

Fortunately, in Morzine it's safe to assume whomever I want to communicate with has a better grasp of English than I do of French (and possibly English too). This is mostly because they're actually English - or French people living in what has become a British colony.

We Brits have a history of expecting foreigners to speak our language and we put little effort into speaking theirs. Even though the British Empire is no more, we still seem to invade other countries and behave as if it did. The French, who also have a history of colonialism, can be a bit touchy about this, having ended up second in the battle for linguistic world supremacy.

Being ashamed of my country's colonial history and a guest in theirs, I try and speak French in France or at least I make a token effort. After my first well-practised sentence, the conversation usually moves to English via Franglais. For those who want to know how it's done, here are my rules of engagement:

1. First you must find a Frenchman. This can be hard in Morzine because 75% of its winter inhabitants are not French. You're mostly likely to find one waiting in a restaurant, behind a bar or till, or wearing ESF ski jackets.
2. When in a restaurant, don't assume that the person standing by your table offering you le menu is French. You can tell if a person is French by their appearance and attitude to service. Simple things, like how a scarf is draped around their neck or the fact they are wearing one indoors, are good indicators. If they've committed a fashion faux pas but appear to have done it on purpose, they're probably French. If they spend an irritating amount of time doing something else before they acknowledge your presence, you can be almost certain they're French.

3. Make sure they know you're English. Your attire and attitude to service can help here too. If, after the initial exchange of *bonjours* (which usually sorts it out), there is still uncertainty, let them make the next move and let them choose the language of first engagement. If there's a double identification mistake, you may well find yourself talking Franglais to a fellow countryman or former colonial and neither party wants that.
4. If you have to make the first salvo, my rules of engagement dictate that you must start off in French; if they're French, you don't want to get off to a bad start. The only thing more insulting to a Frenchman than being mistaken for a Brit, is the assumption that the Frenchman can speak English – even though he probably can. If they're a fourth-generation local, this also reminds them they now live in the English county of Morzineshire.
5. For all the above to work, it's of paramount importance that you rehearse your first line before you enter an establishment, but don't get the accent too perfect otherwise you'll break rule 3. Your interlocutor will then go gibbering on in French until they notice your blank expression. Nine times out of ten you'll get a reply in perfect English and your Franglais encounter will be over.
6. If they want to speak English, let them. I'm not sure if the French in Morzine like to use English to make us feel welcome or simply want to demonstrate their linguistic superiority, or perhaps they just want to practise? It certainly makes me feel guilty, especially after I've just butchered their language with a single sentence. It could just be they are impatient and frustrated after having humoured a dozen grinning English cretins already that day.
7. Avoid a French-Mexican standoff. If you want to practise your French, be mindful of rule 6. I have sat through

many a painful interaction where the waiter insists on speaking English and the diner insists on speaking Franglais. It's like listening to someone on the phone and hearing only half a conversation. They could both be having separate phone conversations for all the sense it makes. The only amusement to be had is betting on who will give up first.

8. There are two main approaches to Franglais; you can choose one or you can mix and match. You can construct sentences in English, but use French nouns (if you know them) or add French conjugation to the English verbs e.g. *'longtemps, pas voir'* *'Fetchez la vache'* and my favourite, *'il* était *un fût de laughs'* (it was a barrel of laughs). Or you can simply reverse the order of the nouns and adjectives. If you don't know the French words simply use the English version e.g. *'ne pas garlic pour moi'* or *'je ne care pas'* or *'c'est not a problème.'*

9. Remember to use *le* and *la*, in front of the English nouns to give them a sex. Just make a stab at the sex of an object. You've got a fifty/fifty chance and who cares what sex a wheelbarrow is anyway? It's **'la** *barrow du roue'* in Franglais in case you're wondering – or *'une brouette'* if you want to use actual French.

10. If you're unlucky, your counterpart might only have a mastery of Frenglish. In which case, you need to simplify your sentences. Things are hot or cold, big or small, good or bad. Don't get too descriptive. You'll know when you've got it right because you'll sound like an apache in a cowboy movie e.g. *'pale face speak with fork tongue'*, *'buffalo gone long time.'*

11. If you've reverted to Frenglish, remember to use excessive inflection at the end of every sentence to make it sound like a question. You'll know when you've got it right because you'll sound like an Australian.

12. If you find yourself speaking Frenglish, don't use colloquialisms. There's enough nonsense in English as it is without trying to explain cockney rhyming-slang. Don't use idioms either. If you say something like '*out of sight out of mind*,' they'll think you're talking about an invisible madman.

If Frenglish isn't an option either, some people revert to Spanglish, having holidayed more in Spain than France. This causes yet further confusion and makes you sound even more of an idiot than any of the above.

13. If you do know the correct French verb, always accompany it with hand gestures or a mime to illustrate it e.g. *manger* must be accompanied with an impression of a hamster eating corn from a cob. *Voiture* (car) needs two oscillating clenched fists and - *le Classique* - an imaginary air-pen must be used when asking for the '*l'addition*' (the bill).
14. Most importantly, always use a comedy '*Allo-Allo*' accent. It probably won't help your Frenchman recognise his own language, but it'll get you in the mood.

If all the above fails and your Franglais, Frenglish or Spanglish is met with a blank expression, simple repeat what you think you said but *louder* and more *slowly* – that usually works.

Ultimately you can just pretend you understand, even if you don't. You do this by saying, '*d'accord*' (okay). If, after being given lengthy directions to the supermarket, you walk off in the wrong direction, imply that you've simply changed your mind. If a perplexed waiter gives up and brings you a plate of beetroot for your main course, just eat it with a happy expression on your face.

I used to dread visiting the French wholesale butchers, just outside of Morzine, where no English was spoken. I had difficulty explaining which cuts of meat I wanted in Franglais – until the butcher created a novel solution to the problem. He bought a farmyard set of toy animals and his non-French-speaking customers would pick one up and point to the part they wanted to eat – genius.

It's often said that French is a much easier language to learn than English because it has a much smaller vocabulary. For instance, the French don't have their own words for *sabotage, renaissance* and *diplomacy* but use ours instead. Their language doesn't accommodate *double-entendres* either. The French can be very *laissez-faire* about numbers too; they don't bother to give anything over sixty its own name. They show little *panache* when naming important items such as the *biscuit*, the *omelette*, a *piste* and other general *bric-a-brac* – it's not a very *entrepreneurial* language at all.

The French often refer to Franglais with disdain. Ironically this is because it means something different to them. In French, Franglais means the excessive use of English phases in French popular culture, e.g. *le weekend, le snack bar, le foot,* and my favourite – *le talkie-walkie (a French walkie-talkie)*.

We have a similar problem with Americanisms slipping into our language. Thanks to the sustained bombardment that is delivered by American TV programmes, terms like 'hyped', 'I'm good', 'rain-check', 'for real' and my least favourite, 'can I get?' have all been assimilated into British English. If anyone asks me, 'can I get?' in the chalet I always answer: 'No you can't, it's not self-service'.

I should really put more effort into learning proper French but every attempt so far has failed. Every time I enrol on a French course, I get faced with verb conjugation and soon give up the task. Despite this, I've learnt quite a few French idioms that amuse me and can be quite useful in my line of work.

The French don't have hangovers; they have a 'face of wood' – *'un visage de bois'*, a useful phrase if you've been 'drinking like a hole' – *'boire comme un trou'*. However, in France, you won't get a 'frog in your throat' but a cat – *'chat dans la gorge'*. If you're feeling faint, you're about to 'fall into the apples' – *'tomber dans les pommes'*. And if your hangover makes you depressed you can tell people you 'have the cockroach' – *'avoir le cafard'*.

You're never an idiot in France; you're 'dumb as a broom' – *'être con comme un balai'*. A Frenchman may think talking to you is a waste of time, like 'pissing in a violin' – *'pisser dans un violon'*. If they don't make a first date, they'll 'send a rabbit' – *'poser un lapin'*. If they fail to keep an appointment, they 'give you the rake' – *'se prendre un râteau'*.

A Frenchman is never big-headed he simple 'farts higher than his arse' – *'péter plus haut que son cul'*. He doesn't sleep around, he 'soaks his biscuit' – *'tremper son biscuit'*. But the French don't make a big fuss about that sort of thing, they 'make a whole cheese' – *'en faire tout un fromage'*.

Given that the ESF would have me arrested if they caught me teaching or leading guests on the snow, people wonder why I haven't moved the Chalet Project to a country with less of a *penchant* for protectionism – or somewhere I can actually speak the local language. I often fail to give a satisfactory answer, but the truth is, I love the French and all their foibles. I love their mountains, their food and of course their wine. I love their culture, their philosophy and humour. I really love their language, despite not being able to speak it and I wish I'd paid more attention in my French classes at school.

9. In Search of Views

During our Jamaican odyssey, my family lived in a house on the hills above Kingston with a breath-taking view of the capital and the ocean beyond - or so I'm told.

Children are very short sighted and don't care, about or notice, views. I was more interested in the exotic insects in the garden and the tree outside my bedroom window that produced enough mangoes to regularly make me sick.

When you grow older you become more long sighted and you start to notice views. You discover that looking at a good view can lift your soul when you're depressed and cool your brow when you're stressed. A proper view can make you forget your problems and cure the most raging of headaches. Good views can replace the images of ugliness you've recently seen with pictures of beauty in your head. Views are always faithful. If you fall in love with a special view, no matter how many times you've seen it before, your heart still swells every time you do. A good view will never let you down. Children don't usually have such emotional requirements.

My father bought a boat and we spent the weekends camping on the islands off Port Royal - snorkelling and spear fishing, a part of my early childhood I remember vividly. But then, without consultation, I was returned to Hull. My parents had their reasons for leaving Jamaica; in particular the escalating crime, perpetrated by some of those who didn't live in houses on hills and have boats.

Living in the UK isn't so bad. At least we don't fear natural disasters. We do have droughts and floods but nothing on a biblical scale: no earthquakes, tsunamis, volcanoes, hurricanes or avalanches to wipe us out while we sleep. There are no dangerous animals other than other humans, and the last civil war was in 1642. In the UK it's mostly safe to go outside. Having said that, it's rather crowded and the weather is rubbish.

It was important to my mother that she had a tree to look at through her window. I didn't really understand this when she first told me, but then I started to have similar emotions about views myself. I wanted to live by water, preferably somewhere by the sea. I've since added mountains, forests and savannahs to my wish list - preferably with a few wildebeest sprinkled amongst them.

After my promising start in Jamaica, I spent my adolescence in South Cave minus a boat, a speargun and one parent. Apart from being the ancestral home of George Washington, South Cave was a bit of a 'nowhere' but it had its charms. It wasn't that far from the sea and it was close to the River Humber (although I had more of a babbling brook in mind for my ideal watery companion, rather than the muddy estuary that is the Humber). South Cave also has some reasonably nice views of the Yorkshire Wolds, if a bit lacking in wildebeest. South Cave may be nowhere but it's my nowhere and I'm still very fond of the place.

I must have inherited my parents' wanderlust, having lived abroad so much myself. Maybe my folks had that common desire to escape their place of birth that a lot of people from Hull seem to have. It could just be the inherent human desire to explore, if only to confirm that the grass isn't greener on the other side of the fence. Some people move aboard simply for better weather; others emigrate for better opportunities or a better lifestyle - or simply because they feel surplus to requirements in the UK. I had many reasons for wanting to live in the Alps, some of which I have forgotten. It might have been that, even though I'd already escaped my place of birth, I'd not found greener pastures. The one reason I do recall for wanting to spend my winters in the mountains was to have better views both from home and at work. Was this reason enough for such a dramatic relocation?

Other practical, social and economic factors are more important to most people than the aesthetic location of their homes. Many people simply accept the location of their birth, tied by family and familiarity. It's easier to build a life in a place where you have roots. Perhaps they lack courage or imagination, or maybe they're just not that fussed about having a decent view.

I left the Hull area again when I was eighteen, this time of my own accord. I lived a student life in a squalid flat in Newcastle. Although I was starting to appreciate views and spent some of my recreational time hiking in the nearby Pennines and the Lakes, nice views weren't a priority then - being near a pub and the University were.

Then I lived wherever I found work, mostly in non-descript places in the Greater London area, none of which were aesthetically better than my place of birth - Hull, and all of them less attractive than the place of my youth - South Cave.

Finally, at the age of twenty-six I escaped the gravitational pull of London. I chose my next location, not for work or for scenery, but for love. I moved to the centre of Birmingham. My future wife, a Brummie, wouldn't live anywhere else.

City living has much to offer. You don't have to catch, kill or even cook your own food. Most things can be delivered to your door. You can walk to work and meet lots of interesting people *en route*. It's easier to make money in cities because all the other people who are trying to make money work there too. The better you get at it, the nearer to the centre you can live and the later you can leave for work. But eventually people who have made enough money and met enough interesting folk, tend to move to the country and champion its virtues - and bang on about the importance of views.

Although I prospered in Brum, put down roots and became attached to many of its inhabitants, the desire for beautiful views started to rear its ugly head. Our apartment looked over a canal basin so I could see water, but there wasn't a tree, let alone a mountain, in sight.

After a couple of hedonistic decades of city living, I started to think Mum was right: sometimes you simply need to look out of your window at a tree. Something I increasingly did although without my wife, in the Alps on holiday. My wife preferred city views and culture to 'fields, sheep, cow shit and heather', as she put it. Although we did do some walking together, it wasn't really her thing.

You're never very far from lakes, trees and mountains in the UK, especially in the North but, thanks to the infrastructure problems we have in England, it takes too long to get to them. It seems like half the population moves north on a Friday and south on a Sunday evening - and don't get me started on bank holiday traffic. Any karma gained from visiting the nice bits of our country is lost during the horrendous journey home. If it all goes smoothly with the flights, it can take less time to get to Morzine, than to drive to North Yorkshire from Birmingham on a Friday.

Not just because of a difference in views on views, my wife and I separated – well, she stayed put and I left. This didn't improve my vista much. I moved into a flat with no view at all - unless you call the living room of the flat opposite a view.

I then moved to Debbie's house in a suburb of Sutton Coldfield, inaccurately named 'Wylde Green' - it wasn't wild in any sense of the word and it didn't have a green. It did have a view of some large, if not mango-laden, trees but I couldn't see water from it nor mountains, and there wasn't a wildebeest in sight.

If you live in suburbia, you have the worst of both worlds. You have none of the benefits of living in the country (fresh air, scenery and silence) and none of the benefits of city living (walking to work, culture and a community) On the other hand, in suburbia you do usually get a garden and plenty of space to park, and your kids get to go to better schools and they don't get mugged on their commute because you drive them there and back.

The good news was that my new love's views on views were much more aligned with my own than my previous love's. However, she had some social and economic issues preventing her from moving somewhere more scenic. She was also a long way behind me on the existential curve – she hadn't even had her midlife crisis yet. She still mostly liked her job and her kids were settled in their schools.

I had moved to the Midlands and prospered, but had not made any aesthetic gains. I was living in someone else's 'nowhere' and it was less scenic than my own 'nowhere'- South Cave.

Wylde Green might not be wild or green, but it had everything a human needed to sustain a comfortable life. Only a man fortunate enough to have first-world problems would be churlish about its view. The more places I've lived the more I realise Hull wasn't such an unfortunate place to be born or Sutton Coldfield such a bad place to live – although I'm still gutted that my parents left Jamaica.

Being spoilt for views in the winter and having seen so many summer alternatives while walking in the North, my desire to live somewhere more scenic was becoming overwhelming.

My biggest problem was how to pull this off, without losing Debbie. I'd already paid the price for my winter views by losing a wife and a home; would I allow my tempestuous love affair with views once again to ruin my life?

Thanks to the geographical lotteries of birth, education and work, most people end up where they end up and just accept their views – unfortunately I'm not one of them.

10. Trigger's Broom

The first time I actually drove a Land Rover Defender was when I rolled Landie off the garage forecourt – well, it was more of a farmyard - near Belbroughton.[14]

I don't know why I'd taken her for a test drive. I had no idea what Defenders were supposed to drive like and if she'd been an old nail or still in the autumn of her youth, I wouldn't have been able to tell. The steering wheel seemed only vaguely connected to the front wheels and the accelerator pedal must have been using semaphore to communicate with the engine.

According to the mechanic who accompanied me, this was all normal and Landie was in rude health. She had the right configuration of seats and a giant roof rack for skis, so I bought her. I shake- rattled-and-rolled my way home while wondering how on Earth I was going to get her all the way to the Alps - and survive the journey myself.

I'd only driven relatively modern cars before. Cars that would have been science fiction when the Defender was first built. I was accustomed to having ABS, active suspension, air-conditioning, in-car entertainment, heated seats and central locking. I'd only driven cars with electric windows and electric everything else. I'd just bought a museum piece with electric nothing - unless you count the interior light.

The most striking thing was the lack of switches and buttons. When I sat in the driving seat of my previous car (a BMW) I had a foreground view of what looked like a plane cockpit; sitting in Landie, the view was more akin to a paddle steamer's bridge.

---

[14] The Defender Centre at Drayton, maintains and resells Defenders. It's a centre of knowledge for, and a shrine to, the vehicle and a source of physical and emotional support for Defender owners.

The Defender is Britain's most famous international movie star and had featured in nearly every action movie I'd ever seen, so I was expecting more obvious signs of greatness. But it's always risky meeting your screen heroes in the flesh especially if they've aged. I knew of the Defender's reputation and the loyalty its enthusiasts had for the brand. However, sitting behind the wheel of a Defender for the first time, made me think they must be a bunch of Luddites who were stuck in the past.

In actual fact, a more metaphorical journey had begun. Six years further down the actual road, I now appreciate the true genius of the Defender's design - given the technology its creators had at their disposal in 1930. My Landie was built in 1996 and a few improvements had been made since the 1930s – a better engine and power steering were added but that was about it. Very little else had been changed and I soon worked out why. For instance, I now know that the gaps at the bottom of the doors are essential for letting out the water that comes in through the gaps at the top. They're just one of many rapid-draining features that I discovered were built into the design.

A rapid-draining vehicle is essential for transporting skiers. Skiers bring lots of snow into the vehicle on their boots, which soon melts and the resulting water must go somewhere – usually though the rust holes in the floor. Eight skiers will also exhale a lot of water vapour - they're usually hot and breathing heavily when they get in. The bare metal roof condenses this vapour quickly and cools the skier by dripping it down his or her neck. It always seems to be raining inside Landie even if there isn't a cloud in the sky.

Thanks to all that inconsiderate breathing, I have to de-ice the inside of Landie's windows along with the outside most mornings. Particularly in February, liberating Landie from snow and ice can be a laborious task if I don't go through her bedtime routine correctly. I learnt, in Season 1, that locking the doors in the evenings was a mistake because the locks froze solid overnight. I bought a special device for injecting de-icer into them but I stupidly kept locking it inside the vehicle. On those occasions, when I finally managed to get the doors open, the mechanism still being frozen, they usually wouldn't latch shut again so I would have to hold one door closed with the other by strapping a bungee between their handles across the front passengers' laps.

Landie's bedtime routine used to involve the removal of her fuel filter to store it somewhere warm in the chalet overnight. This stopped the diesel in it waxing, a condition that prevented her from starting in the morning. It also compensated for the lack of door security by disabling the engine. It did mean I smelt vaguely of diesel most of the day - or of *'eau de Land Rover'* as it's called in Franglais.

During February Season 2 we had some freakish weather in Morzine and the temperature fell so low that with wind-chill, the thermometer was frequently reading below -20°c at night. Landie, like just about every other vehicle not stored in a garage, froze solid. I looked for a solution on the internet and discovered that in Siberia they warm the fuel lines on their Defenders with a blowtorch and even light a fire under the fuel tank! Given that this might alarm my guests if I tried it, my solution was to share my accommodation, the garage, with Landie until the cold snap was over. It was a bit of a squeeze, man and machine bedded down together, but each night I drove Landie into the garage then slept in her back.

I subsequently discovered a fuel additive that stops diesel waxing below -18°c and now I always pay the extra for winter diesel even if it's not especially cold, in case the weather changes before it's time to fill up again. To survive freak weather, you've always got to be prepared for the worst.

If waterproofness (rather than water tightness) is one of the Defender's main design triumphs then mechanical simplicity is its other. Instead of automatic traction control it has a second small gear stick that allows the axle differential to be manually locked. This means you can make all four wheels spin at once in the hope that one of them will find some grip. It's also used to engage the low ratio gears in case you want to drive up a cliff.

Passengers often ask me, 'What does that little knob do?' This leads me to crack a couple of well-rehearsed *double-entendres* then give a lengthy explanation of what an axle differential does and why it's disadvantageous when driving in snow - it also leads them to regret having ever asked.

This simplicity of a Defender means even I can understand how Landie works. It's reassuring to lift the bonnet and see something you recognise as an engine and know what all the discrete parts do. Under the bonnet of a modern car all you'll find is alien technology best left well alone. Modern vehicles are now engineered for ease and cost of manufacture, rather than for ease of maintenance by a numpty in the field. Theoretically, the Defender's well-understood simplicity means that any problems can be diagnosed and fixed by an amateur mechanic. All you need is a Haynes Manual, a socket set, a hammer, a role of gaffer tap and a can of WD40.

Knowing the purpose of all the components makes me feel like a sports physiotherapist and an essential part of the mechanical team. For instance, having stripped down and rebuilt the door-window mechanism, I feel a sense of satisfaction when winding it up and down. I visualise the cogs and leavers in motion and sometimes mimic the non-existent motor by making a humming sound.

10. TRIGGER'S BROOM

In a very confusing world, where the purpose of life is unclear, it's good to understand, or at least feel you understand, how a closed system, like Landie, works. Within the universe between her four wheels, there are no mysteries or paradoxes to be solved. There are no unknown forces working for good or evil, just cogs, nuts and bolts, each with a well-understood purpose. The only price you pay for this good feeling is reliability and even then, if well maintained, Defenders seldom grind to a complete halt.

There's a downside of course – anxiety. You don't have to understand modern cars to drive them – most of them just invariably work. We rely on faith, not knowledge of what's under their bonnet and assume, when we turn the key, they will always start and take us to work. Having a reliable vehicle is of paramount importance for my job of delivering an enjoyable skiing holiday to my guests. Too much knowledge of the interior workings can undermine my faith and I'm always unduly worried that Landie will conk out (knowledge always seems to undermine a man's faith). However, given the mileage I do, it's not that often that she lets me down. I've always believed it's better to rely on knowledge rather than faith – but that was always going to be a more stressful approach to life.

In the early days of ownership I tried to fix Landie's many rattles and squeaks, but every time I tracked down and fixed one, a new one would chirp up. Now I realise Landie was simply trying to communicate using the language of percussion. New noises and indeed smells come and go, you just have to hum along to every new beat. In a modern car, a single rattle can drive you to distraction but for some reason, when dozens of them form a cacophony, they don't.

I do worry about the impact my diesel guzzler has on the environment. However, Landie has lasted much longer than most other cars, which invariably end up being scrapped. Even the oldest hybrid hasn't yet paid back the environmental cost of its build. Landie may be a polluter but she's made efficient use of the metal consumed in her creation.

I feel annoyed that, because of her emissions, the UK road tax for Landie is so high and, because most of my mileage is done in France, that the wrong exchequer is getting my dosh. I would also like it noted that my overall environmental impact is very low compared to those driving electric cars if they have kids.

The true joy of owning a Defender is that there's always something to investigate and fix. When you buy one you've got yourself a new hobby whether you wanted it or not. It's a hobby that keeps on giving and after seven years, I've changed so many components on Landie (some twice) that I'm thinking of renaming her Trigger's Broom.

On one occasion, I noticed that Landie was leaking fuel, but not enough to worry about, and set off to collect my guests. They were at an open-air concert near Prodains. The area was packed with après revellers, but I managed to squeeze Landie into a parking space next to the stage. I joined my guests and forgot about the leak and started enjoying the show. That was until a bunch of fire-eating go-go girls jumped on the stage and started cavorting, throwing sparks in every direction. I rushed back to Landie and drove swiftly away from the stage, leaving a trail of diesel behind me. I kept anxiously checking in my mirror that I wasn't being following by a line of fire. There's never a dull moment when you drive a Defender.

There are those who pimp their Land Rovers and spend hours polishing and admiring but they're missing the *raison-d'être* of a Land Rover. A Defender should be off-road somewhere, wheel-arch deep in mud, not gleaming on a suburban drive.

It's always a mistake to hoover inside a Defender, because you'll lose too many important, yet-to-be-identified-as-missing nuts and bolts. Ultimately, if you take a Defender down the pimping road, you'll just end up driving a really crap car.

Being a vintage model there are no unnecessary electrical items in my Landie, which means less stuff to fix or indeed malfunction when wet. In later models things like electric windows, central locking and air conditioning were added which, in my opinion, perverted the essence of the classic design.

I like to tell younger passengers, who haven't encountered manual windows before, that Landie is a free gym and that the windows are one of the many pieces of exercise equipment it contains. The workout starts when you pull-up on the doorframe and use the steps to climb in. And during the journey your biceps get a good workout holding on to whatever solid fixture you can find.

Landie's seats are good for your posture because it's impossible to slouch in what are basically kitchen chairs. The rear ladder is designed to improve core body strength while loading and unloading skis.

The heavy clutch gives the driver's left quadriceps a good workout too. Strong quads are essential for skiing, but unfortunately the asymmetry in leg strength I've developed in the Land Rover Gym has caused me some problems on the piste. It's made my right carved turn stronger than my left and given me a propensity to ski in circles. Anyway, enough about skiing.

Depending on where you sit in a Landie, you get a different experience. Being an ex-M.O.D. vehicle, she has bench seats in the back. This means riding in the back is a very sociable experience. Rear passengers sit facing each other in military fashion and to prevent being thrown around, it's best if they interlock their knees. They can't see where they're heading, which is usually for the best, and are forced to make conversation.

For those riding shotgun, the front seat offers a slightly more comfortable ride along with an external view. However, sitting in the front means you might have to endure a lecture on differential locks from me. I often allocate the front seat on compassionate grounds to the injured, the carsick or to whoever has learnt to shout 'shotgun' first.

I once made a serving British Army general, who didn't qualify on any of the above grounds, sit in the back. While climbing into the rear with the rest of the troops, he jokingly complained, 'Chris, I usually sit in the front of these'. I told him his rank counted for nothing in Morzine and that he was in my skiing army now.

Once, midseason, I had to drive a modern hybrid hire car for a guest and it proved challenging. Firstly, I got into the passenger side forgetting continental cars are left-hand drive. After checking no one was looking, I got out and back in on the side that had the steering wheel. I looked around for somewhere to insert the key but there wasn't a slot to be found, just a start button. I pressed it and nothing happened. Then I discovered it was running in electric mode. I then found the hand brake and it too was a button. I pressed it but it wouldn't disengage until I'd depressed the foot brake. I began to wonder if the car was more intelligent than me. It was an automatic, so there was no clutch to worry about. I pressed the accelerator – a conventional foot pedal and it finally started to hover forward. Compare to Landie, it was like piloting a spaceship – I didn't like it one bit.

10. TRIGGER'S BROOM

I'm always terrified when I drive a rental car that I may scratch it and lose my deposit. This also reminds me how liberated Landie makes me feel, not having to care about her paintwork. I also prefer to feel intellectually superior to the vehicles that I drive.

Most things on Landie can be unbolted and replaced including most of the body panels. I never repair her external scars because I'm likely to dent the same panel again. I also like to think these flesh wounds give her character and are an important historic record of battles won against snowdrifts, hedges and gateposts. They also serve as a warning to other drivers to always give way. Anyway, if I had money to waste on cosmetic surgery, I'd probably spend it on myself.

The longer you own a Defender and the more stuff you've had to fix, the more intimate the relationship becomes. Even if I win the lottery, I suspect Landie will be the last vehicle I'll ever buy. She suits my new existential philosophy of not caring what other people think – I'll decide, and no one else, if I'm a loser because I drive a beat-up old van.

I prefer to think I'm driving a classic that's still today the best form of transport in mountainous terrain. Maybe I'm simply driving a relic from the age that I would have preferred to belong to. Either way, despite all the fancy cars I've owned and driven in the past, I'm finally driving a company car I can be proud of – even if it comes with a low paid job.

When I first drove that rubbish vehicle from that farmyard in Belbroughton, I didn't realise how attached I'd become to her or how much she would test my faith. It turned out she suited most of my physical and philosophical needs – if not my mental health ones.

11. The Agents of Entropy

Scientifically speaking, entropy is a thermodynamic quantity representing the unavailability of a system's thermal energy for conversion into mechanical work, often interpreted as the degree of disorder or randomness in the system. It's also a fundamental law of thermodynamics: that any closed system evolves toward a state of maximum entropy.

I believe the forces that create entropy are constantly working on me. I'll save you from my full thesis on the subject, which I'll admit has its scientific flaws, but I've noticed that the thermodynamic system called 'my life' tends to a state of disorder and I constantly lose irretrievable energy trying to prevent it from falling into chaos.

I may not be alone in this. For example, have you noticed how a house becomes untidy all on its own? Objects don't just leap out of the cupboards, something or someone, has used energy to move them and you must deploy an equal amount of energy to put them back. In the thermodynamic system known as 'a chalet' this is a constant process and the energy used is entropic, it cannot be reused for constructive purposes – it's gone forever. I call the 'somethings and someones' the 'Agents of Entropy' and I've unwittingly been at war with them all my life.

Most of the Agents are human, although some appear in animal form, usually disguised as domestic pets. Others are mental constructs, like the Ski Demons, that cause disorder and a lot of heat in my head. Some are simply forces of nature (extreme weather) or the passage of time (ageing) that destroy the order we humans create.

Chalet guests are the most common Agents of Entropy in my universe, especially if they've had a drink. Some are worse than others: the feckless, the bad timekeepers, the accident-prone and those who always seem to get into a scrape.

Children start out as Agents and don't need the influence of drink. But some get better at fighting for order once they've been through that teenage Agents of Anarchy stage.

Even well-disciplined adults can temporarily become Agents, especially when they go on holiday. I think it's called letting your hair down or reliving your youth. Such Agents have a tendency to leave their stuff all over the chalet or randomise the molecules of a glass or plate by dropping it onto the floor. If I'm forced to enter their rooms mid-stay, I'll often find towels, clothes and other, often unsavoury, items scattered all over the place. But I don't wonder if we've had burglars; I just know that an Agent of Entropy has been at work.

Interestingly, when I show guests to their rooms, men will usually mark their territory by dumping their suitcases on their allocated bed then immediately return to the living area to drink beer. They never unpack, but take items out of their cases when they're needed. Women, however usually disappear for at least an hour and unpack their bags, utilising the room's storage furniture and setting up their toiletries in the bathroom – and heaven knows what else. Given this difference in gender behaviour, it's interesting that the laws of thermodynamics are not sexist and by the end of their stay nearly all the rooms look like a burglar has been through them. Anyway, enough about sexual stereotypes – it's got me into too much trouble before.

The most prolific Agents are the clumsy and the impatient. They work away at the fabric of the chalet. You could call it wear-and-tear, but there's a never-ending list of maintenance issues I have to waste entropic energy rectifying. Showers, windows, door-handles and kitchen devices seemingly malfunction all on their own. Not a day goes by when I don't have to replace or repair something and I'm staggered by the number of toilet seats I've had to fix/replace since the Chalet Project began – what on Earth are people doing in there?

I've devised a simple test to identify the Agents of Entropy, which I call the 'French Door' test. If a guest can consistently operate French door furniture without breaking it, they're safe to leave on their own (more about the French Door Test later).

Some friends are worse Agents than others and whenever they come into my life an increase in disorder, if not chaos, is usually the result. They can lead me to change sides and engage in entropic activity myself. I sometimes think I become a double Agent of Entropy when I've done something stupid or self-destructive, or something that cannot be undone, or said something I didn't mean that can't be unsaid.

The worst Agent of Entropy is time. It has a slow but unstoppable effect on the randomness of the human body. I have to put an ever-increasing amount of energy into biological maintenance – by eating well and keeping fit enough to do battle with the other Agents.

The alpine weather is a powerful Agent too. Wind, snow and ice cause chaos and disorder, blocking roads and bursting pipes and avalanches are particularly good at randomising stuff that gets in their way. No matter how much we humans create order, a violent storm or biblical flood can mix everything up again.

I'm undecided if Mother Nature herself is an Agent of Entropy: ivy attacks our walls and tree roots undermine our foundations. Then again, living things are highly structured in a biological sense. She can organise oxygen, carbon, hydrogen, nitrogen and calcium atoms in some amazingly complicated ways. Maybe she has a different definition of order. Humans order things in straight lines and separate them into groups, but Mother Nature's idea of 'order' is higgledy-piggledy and evenly mixed up. Anyway, that's enough about gardening.

Entropy's agents often like to work together which is why bad things happen in threes. Landie always breaks down when I'm trying to fix something else and then a 'someone or something' misplaces my phone. I've also noticed that the Agents wait until I've got a hangover before springing their coordinated attacks.

The Agents of Entropy work on a macro as well as a microscopic scale. Empires fall, civilisations collapse and humans, like the dinosaurs, will eventually become extinct. The Earth itself is on a march towards randomness and will eventually be consumed by the sun. If you view a life, a chalet, a planet or a solar system as a closed thermodynamic entity, then you know that the war for order cannot ultimately be won. Everything we build will be broken, grown over, eroded and, sooner rather than later, we too will be turned into dust.

I know that believing in supernatural entities masquerading as humans, makes me sound like David Icke, but my conspiracy theory is based on science. I've simply extended the laws of thermodynamics to explain the chaos that goes on in my life. You may have suspected that forces beyond your control have been working against you all your life too – well now you can give them a collective name.

12. Ski Like Nobody is Watching

I've never liked going to ski school. Well, that's not exactly true. I was looking forward to going to my first beginners' class, but once I'd realised the enormity of the task ahead (just after I put my skis on), I was demoralised.

Initially I thought they'd put me in the wrong class. Everyone, apart from me, had some ability to remain erect on skis while moving but every time I tried to move, I fell over. I soon discovered it was a class of frauds and most had been skiing before. They should have called it the 'nervous ninnies and consolidators' class – they'd obviously learnt the most important lesson in skiing: never be T.E. Charlie - the weakest skier in a group.

I said to Ingrid, my first instructor (I'm not counting the hung-over Geordies), 'can you find me an *actual* beginners' class?' She pointed at the toddlers in the kindergarten area, hanging onto plastic penguin stabilisers bigger than themselves. I laughed at her supposed joke. At that point in our relationship, I hadn't realised that she was a humourless ice-maiden. My only consolation was that being the class dunce gained me a lot of sympathy. I also gained a female admirer who presumably found lost causes, especially those dripping in sweat, attractive.

After that, I preferred to take private lessons with actual English instructors, not simply English-speaking ones. Fellow countrymen can communicate with you at a deeper level, using sarcasm, humour and obscenity in a shared mother tongue. To be fair to Ingrid, her English was very good and, being British, I hadn't bothered to learn any of her mother tongue (German) apart from a few phrases I learnt from comic books and war movies which, even then, would probably have been politically incorrect to use - although I was tempted.

My problem, when it comes to learning, is an inability to listen - despite having two ears and one mouth. I've always maintained that it's a comprehension issue, not a listening one, and I don't want to appear thick by admitting I don't understand.

I find it hard to assimilate the avalanche of information most instructors provide. When you go for one lesson, they tend to cover the entire gamut of skiing instead of explaining one or two simple aspects.

I also have difficulty focusing on more than one thing at once – I am male after all. There's quite a lot to remember when adopting the *right* skiing posture. I'll be focusing on holding my arms out and at the recommended elevation, but then I forget to bend from the waist, while holding my head up and rotating from the hips while pressing on my big toe. Skiing, the BASI way at least, is a bit like playing Twister.[15]

According to my instructors, I have a lot of bad habits. After a couple of decades of skiing I've picked up quite a few of them and they are ingrained in my muscle memory. If I shake off one bad habit it comes back when I'm trying to get rid of another. The minute I stop concentrating on my posture I revert back to being a skiing slob.

It's hard teaching someone to ski using any system, because skiing is so counterintuitive – for most of us anyway. You have to lean down the slope, toward the danger, not away from it; if you lean back, you speed up and if you lean forward, you slow down. It's the opposite of running. To turn left, you need to lean right, to turn right you need to lean left – it's all messed up.

---

15 For those who have never played a game requiring more than thumb movement, **Twister** was a game theoretically designed to make players contort in amusing positions. However it ended up facilitating most of my generation's first sexual encounter and involved much more intimate contact with the opposite sex than Grand Theft Auto ever will.

Nobody ever taught us to walk, we just worked it out, and our parents didn't make us wear helmets either. Imagine trying to teach 'walking' to a one-year-old. First you'd explain the principles of Newtonian physics then a bit of gravitational theory – which is going to be tricky given their vocabulary. You'd underline the importance of arm movements despite walking being done with the legs and generally confuse the hell out of them. Once they'd got their level 1 walking badge, they could move up to level 2 (running) through an intermediary perambulating technique called skipping.

I also get bored easily. Unless the instructor is a talented entertainer I start looking at my watch or the scenery. I'm not used to skiing for more than a couple of hours without a sit down and a chat about something non-skiing related. The mechanics of skiing isn't actually that fascinating to me and once I've lost the thread of the lesson, if indeed there was one, I switch off.

Group lessons can be especially boring if one of your fellow students isn't too embarrassed to admit his stupidity. Such students will demonstrate their lack of comprehension by asking seemingly random questions about skiing, unrelated to the exercise in hand. If it's a more advanced group, the class swot can become annoying as well, by giving their own advice to the group. Meanwhile you're standing around, in painful boots, trying not to add to the confusion by adding your own less helpful observation: 'I'm paying him to teach me; not to listen to you.'

We all have our own methods of learning. Some like to have a discussion, ask questions, challenge the answers and get everything sorted in their minds first; some like to jump in, have a go, get it wrong, and then learn why. I need diagrams.

Most instructors try and explain the complex dynamics between arms, legs, hips, toes and skis using only words and, if you're lucky, the odd squiggle in the snow. In my opinion, all ski lessons should start in a classroom with a blackboard.

It would also help to have an artist's mannequin to confirm that my own skeleton works in a conventional way. People are generally unaware of how their skeleton works and what muscles they use to control it. For instance, the cognitive process for taking a drink goes like this: 'I think I'll pick up that pint glass'. That's it. After that, an arm and the attached hand just do it for you. No specific orders need to be given to the fingers or thumb, nor indeed any of the fifty-odd muscles involved in successful acquisition of the pint. Obviously, if repeated too often, the mouth has to move towards the glass to shorten the distance and our body even does this automatically – it's wonderful to watch.

Like most, I get very self-conscious when I know someone is watching me. I try too hard and usually start cocking things up. I over-think what I'm doing and put my brain, rather than my body, in charge. Sometimes I just say to myself, 'Ski like nobody is watching.' If I do that, I usually get better results.

Having owned them since I was a small boy, I've become very attached to my limbs, but I'm still very unaware of their exact orientation at any given time. Most humans only have a vague notion of what their limbs are up to, while they're trying to do something else. The best way to check your deportment is by looking at your own reflection - which is why ballerinas practise in dance studios with walls covered in mirrors. I think my skiing classroom should be similarly equipped. Having said that, I normally avoid mirrors, preferring my mental self-image to the truth – in my mind I'm young, thin and have hair.

Another issue (I admit, they're building up) is inconsistency between instructors. They all have their own variations in teaching methodology or so it seems, and they often give contradictory advice. You latch onto something from one lesson, that seems to really work, shoulders square to the fall line for instance. Then, a couple of years later, you're told to face in the direction of travel. Fashions change, along with the shape and size of skis. What a good skier looks like seems to evolve and all of a sudden good habits become bad ones. Maybe I just need to wait until all my bad habits become fashionable again. I may have a long wait.

Most instructors have developed a set of skiing drills that they think are helpful for students like me – the students with learning difficulties. These usually involve skiing without poles, skiing with boots undone, skiing with one ski in the air and other such hazardous acrobatics. They're supposed to help hone a specific skill but we all know they're really created so the instructor can show off. Here are some I've remembered:

1. Punching the Dwarf. Designed to exaggerate a waist-level fist movement that helps to initiate a turn. It might also help you to improve your chances of surviving a conflict in Middle Earth.
2. Burka Skiing. Hold your poles together horizontally, arms outstretched and try and see the tips of your skis through the gap between them. I can't remember what it's supposed to do for your skiing – I was too busy laughing at the time.
3. John Wayne Skiing. Try to imagine you're on a horse; this helps to get the leg separation correct. Pretending basketballs, ripe tomatoes, sea urchins and other round objects are between your legs seems very popular too.
4. Psychopath Mogul Killer. This involves stabbing moguls in the head with your pole then slitting their throats with

your skis. There aren't many ways to make mogul-skiing fun, but this one helps. 'Die moguls, die'.
5. Mick Jagger Skiing. The perfect hip movement for skiing has been described as a 'mince'. Face contortions are optional, unless you really want to throw yourself into the role.
6. Dumpski. This involves pretending you're using a French toilet (the hole-in-the-ground type). This improved my snowploughing no end.

The other kind of instructor I like, and they're usually French, is the kind that relates everything to the Kama Sutra. I find this approach very educational, and sometimes it improves my skiing too. However, it was an English instructor who once described the ideal knee movement as 'tea-bagging' which I had to Google when I got home (as you're probably doing right now).

The more vulgar a description, the more the mental image is engrained in my mind. Unfortunately, this means I'm often thinking about sex when I'm skiing and, even more worryingly, the other way round.

The other type of instructor I enjoy skiing with, although they don't necessarily improve my skiing, I call the Jedi Masters. They tell you to 'be one with the snow,' or 'don't think, use The Force'. One told me that the spiritual being can be separated from the physical one and suggested I made my spiritual being ski ten metres in front of me - I think he was trying to make me lean forward more. Another told me he used Neuro-Linguistic Programming techniques, which made the conversation on the chairlifts fascinating, but his Jedi mind tricks didn't work on me.

The instructors I try to avoid are the ones who bombard me with criticism, however humorously or constructively couched. I understand that instructors of any discipline need to point out things that you're doing wrong, but sometimes I feel they're a little nit-picky. They have a need to find something (or just anything) that needs improving to justify their fee and ensure your return. I've never heard of a ski instructor telling his pupil, 'You ski perfectly,' then ending the lesson – it's certainly never happened to me.

Which brings me to the biggest issue I have with all this academic work. What's the difference between a good skier and a bad skier? If, after a planned manoeuvre, both end up standing where they intended, then who is the better skier? The difference is simply a matter of speed and grace. We're all falling down the mountain, it's just some of us look like we're ballerinas and some of us don't. There is no wrong way of doing it - you can't really do anything *wrong* on skis if what you do works.

Now that I'm supposedly a good skier (whatever that means), I have another issue that makes ski lessons and drills particularly tiresome. Criticism is often prefixed with the words, 'at your level, you should be able to …', which implies I'm not the only person with doubts about how I got my instructor's badge and blue jacket. I should be able to do all the drills well - but I can't and frankly it's embarrassing.

I don't believe in the proverb, 'those who can, do; those who can't, teach,' but my own version of it - 'those who can, do - but shouldn't necessarily teach' – is better. If you find something easy you often struggle to explain why. If you've struggled to master something, then succeeded, you've probably constructed and destructed the problems you encountered many times. The best teacher is often the one who was once rubbish himself. Anyway, enough of my sales pitch.

Given that I can already ski any marked piste in any condition (at least the ones I've come across so far) and that I can go reasonably fast, usually, without falling, why do I want to be a BASI ballerina? Why do I keep going to ski lessons if I find them such torture?

I go because, despite the embarrassment, confusion and demoralisation, I usually get one great tip, one piece of advice that my legs remember, or one unsavoury mental image that I can think about when I'm skiing with nobody watching.

13. Angry Pirates

It was 4am and the only alcohol left in the chalet was a bottle of Malibu. The bottle was of unknown origin and had, for four seasons, been rejected in favour of just about anything else - but now was its time. Nobody wanted to go to bed, so we opened it.

In Charlie's case, there was little point in going to bed because his transfer to the airport was in two hours' time. David had more time, an extra day, but, for once, I doubted he would make the first lift.

I'd invited the Morzine International Ladies Federation (MILFs), including Morzine Mary, round for paella – my signature dish. The MILFs knew how to party and so did David and Charlie.

To add to the international ambience, we were listening to Radio Dos, a Puerto Rican internet radio station, that plays English rock classics and there had already been some serious Dad Dancing. Liz's dog, Doodle, had been ready to go bed several hours earlier, but she lay quietly in front of the fire. She'd seen it all before.

I'd seen it all before too, but it had been a while since I'd engaged in a full-on session and, being with friends, I wasn't too worried about the Après Aliens gate-crashing the party. Charlie was an old colleague from my days working as a marketing whore and he had similar opinions about the industry and those who inhabit it, and bitching about it and them was therapy for both of us.

David was getting a few days skiing in without his wife. He'd relaxed his *carpe-diem* attitude towards skiing since his retirement: he could go skiing whenever he liked. Perhaps David was especially chilled that night because we'd spent all day skiing the Donkey's Knob!

13. ANGRY PIRATES

The area below the *Cornebois* peak of *Châtel* is known as the Donkey's Knob. A lot of popular off-piste routes have English nicknames, perhaps because the French names are too difficult for us to pronounce in Franglais. The slang names are usually more descriptive and therefore more memorable, however, no matter how much I squint at *Cornebois*, I've never seen a rock structure resembling a phallus – donkey shaped or otherwise. I conclude that rather than it being a physically descriptive name it must be an expression of joy. The area has many gullies safe from avalanche, making it the dog's bollocks for off-piste beginners. Maybe 'donkey's knob' is simply one superlative up from the 'dogs' bollocks'? Anyway, back to the party.

I'd thrown the dinner-come-dance party in celebration of a great opening week to Season 5. The snow had arrived mercifully after the successful, if not uneventful, Bacon Run.[16] I'd quickly settled back into my winter home and was once again living the dream. I had no idea it was going to be my last season in Chalet Neige; I was simply enjoying the skiing and enjoying having friends, rather than paying guests, in the chalet – although they still contributed cash and I still did the cooking, it didn't feel the same.

After another long summer, it was great to be back in the Alps with my hedonistic friends. I was still celebrating the ownership of my blue jacket and I probably put it on at some stage – it had yet to be worn in action. Also, after four seasons of pretending to be a chalet-cook, a chalet-host and a ski-guide, I felt like I was now the genuine article. My bookings diary for the season was

---

16 I call my journey from the UK to the Alps the **Bacon Run** because my most important cargo is English bacon. I discover that others us the same name for their winter migration - for similar reasons.

full and the Project was going from strength to strength. I'd found ways round most of the chalet's foibles and indeed those of my regular guests so nothing much fazed me anymore.

Mercifully, there were no Angry Pirates at the party. Charlie had introduced me to the drink the previous season; it consisted of a shot of Captain Morgan's rum with a slice of lemon on the side. I remember enquiring why it was called an 'Angry Pirate' and not just 'rum'. He squeezed the lemon into his eye, put his hand over it, downed the rum then involuntarily hopped around the chalet screaming 'aaargh' and I realised why. Needless to say, we all had a go.

That night, I suggested it might work just as well with Malibu and started looking for a lemon. However, Charlie had learnt his lesson and no longer plundered the alcoholic seas. He recalled the last time we'd been Angry Pirates together and his horrendous journey home accompanied by a hangover from the Caribbean.

The older I get the more brutal and enduring are my hangovers. There are many physiological reasons for the amplifications but, basically, old bodies take longer to recover. Frankly, when you're fifty-plus, you don't feel particularly well most of the time and a hangover doesn't really help. Worse than the physical symptoms are the psychological ones. I enter what I now know is called, the 'prison of existential self-loathing' and the older I get, the longer the sentence and the thicker the prison bars become.

I'd empathised with Charlie, having made so many painful retreats from the Alps, via Geneva Airport (GVA) myself, and I put the bottle of Malibu away and we compared notes on hangover-journeys. The journey usually goes something like this:

13. ANGRY PIRATES

At some ungodly hour, you climb into the transfer van tired, dehydrated and still partially inebriated. Your body is aching in unfamiliar places thanks to the battering you've given it on the slopes and you're a little resentful that the transfer company is picking you up so early. Worried about traffic, they think it might take longer than an hour to drive to GVA and that you do *actually* need to be at the airport two hours before your take off time. You'd lied about your departure time to get another thirty minutes in bed - but it's still stupid-o-clock.

The van is often filled with similarly grumpy, battered and hung-over pirates, sweating and billowing alcohol fumes. If you're unlucky (which I usually am) there will be a screaming baby or a child who gets carsick amongst them. If you're *really* unlucky, there'll be a chirpy morning person wanting to chat.

It will soon become clear if the driver is going for the Morzine-to-GVA speed record. And he's keen to move up the Man-in-a-Reasonably-Priced-Van leader-board back in the office. The racetrack has several vomit inducing bends and you start to hope that you encounter traffic that will force him to slow down. If you're lucky the driver is female.

The best place to sit is in the front. It gives you a good view of the upcoming road and enough time to say a little prayer each time Lewis Hamilton decides to overtake on a blind bend even though he assures you he's checked the bend was clear through a gap in the trees.

The danger in securing the front seat is that the driver may be a talker. But if you do engage, you run the risk of having to answer the groundhog questions or indeed, out of politeness, ask them yourself. To reduce the conversational effort for both, it's sometimes best to shut your eyes and pretend you've fallen asleep - however this exacerbates your nausea. If you sit in the back, you'll spend the journey feeling sorry for the passengers sitting shoulder to shoulder with a, still fairly angry, pirate.

If the passengers are old, they may ask the driver to turn the heating up. You may be desperate to open a window and get some fresh air, but you won't. If the driver is young and not a talker, he may start playing loud grunge music on the vehicle's stereo. You assume they're doing this to keep themselves awake - they surely can't be listening to it for pleasure; you're tempted to ask for it to be turned down (or preferably off) - but you don't want to take the risk.

If you do encounter traffic, you start to worry about missing your flight and you regret lying about your take-off time. If Lewis is driving, and there's no traffic, someone will be sick. You then have to concentrate harder on not blowing chunks yourself. If one child blows, his brother will soon join him, closely followed by you.

If there's no traffic, you arrive at the airport three hours early to find your flight has been delayed - because planes are never delayed when you're running late.

Common reasons given for flights being delayed are: 'technical problems' (plane failure), air-traffic or baggage-handler strikes and bad weather - of all the airports in the world, you'd have thought GVA would know how to deal with snow. Finally there's the catchall excuse: 'Due to earlier delays...' We all know the budget airline model has no slack in its capacity, and they'd be more honest telling us: 'Your plane is delayed because your seats were too cheap.'

Now the rollercoaster ride is over, your feelings of nausea subside and are replaced with feelings of paranoia. You know there *will* be a large and slow moving queue at the check-in desk and an even bigger one at security. You know the security staff *will*

pick on you for a full-body search. Your flight *will* be cancelled, your bags *will* get lost and you *will* lose your passport. The Agents of Entropy know you've got a hangover and you know that they *will* twist the knife.

You check you have your passport, wallet and phone every five minutes and go into panic every time they're not in the pocket you thought they were in. It's important to remember that just because you're paranoid, it doesn't mean everyone isn't out to get you.

You thank the transfer driver (if you're not English, with a tip) then take a brief gasp of crisp winter air and step into the tropical world of GVA. By now, you are seriously regretting not taking a bottle of water with you on the transfer van and you're on a mission to rehydrate.

I'm not sure why GVA is kept so hot in the winter. Most of the passengers are going skiing and are dressed accordingly. Most usually have sun or windburn on the way back. I suspect the heat boosts sales of water, which you'll pay any price for once you're captive in the airport. Mercifully, I now have access to the executive lounge, which is literally an oasis in the desert.

Having endured the check-in queue and said goodbye to your bag, you drag your skis to the other end of the terminal and say a last farewell to them. You know you'll never see them again but you're not that bothered – you'll probably never go skiing again. Unburdened, you can now focus on finding water - but you need to get through security first.

If you are running late, it seems like everyone in front of you hasn't flown since 9/11. They act surprised when asked to take most of their clothes off before going through the x-ray machine.

When you finally get air-side and have re-dressed, you'll find the nearest water outlet and hand over a fifty-Euro note, forgetting that they'll give you change in Swiss Francs and the change will end up in your man drawer and you'll forget to take it with you next year. Fortunately, if you're also ordering a rubber sandwich, there won't be much of it.

Once you've added water to your system, like a dry sponge, your medial temporal lobe will rapidly inflate and memories of the previous evening will start flooding back. Worrying sound-bytes from your drunken conversations drift in through your prison bars along with flashbacks from the previous night that would make a Roman banquet look tame.

You feel guilty and wander around the duty-free shops looking for a present for your wife, one you can actually afford. You settle on a giant bar of Toblerone, which you'll end up eating most of yourself when she finally gets to open it.

Your gate number comes up and you start the considerable walk towards it. It *will* be changed at the last minute. Then, despite having arrived three hours early at the airport, you'll end up running to the new gate while listening to your name being called out on the tannoy. Well, you think it's your name; the woman on the microphone is unintelligible thanks to an accent that makes German, French and English all sound identical.

If they don't change the gate, you'll have plenty of time to sit, or more likely stand because there are never enough seats, and reflect on your life. You begin to wonder if squeezing lemon into your own eye was simply to amuse others or that you subconsciously enjoy self-harming.

Debbie recently discovered the best way to get through GVA is in a wheel chair. You're pushed to the front of every queue and always have a seat on hand. Better still, they allocate you a porter to carry your bags and generally take all responsibility for getting you on the right plane. They will carry you up the stairs onto the plane and give you an entire row of seats to lie across. 'It was almost worth getting injured for,' she claimed.

Whilst sat at the gate you eye-up your fellow-passengers for potential troublemakers. On the way out you were looking for stag/hen parties, but going home such skiing tribes are always subdued. You scan for babies, small kids and fat people. If there are any, you know that they *will* have been allocated the seats next to you.

Most importantly, are there any people who look like they might have recently been angry seafarers? You really don't want to sit next to someone sweating and smelling like you do. It's easy to tell an ex-angry pirate, because only one of their eyes will be bloodshot.

Now your temporal lobe is fully inflated, paranoia is replaced with depression. Memories of other alcohol-related incidents add to your existential self-loathing. You've been here many times before and you're not just referring to the airport.

Everyone else has anxiety that there will not be enough locker space for their hand luggage, but you refuse to join the *melée* on principle, so you wait until the very last minute to get on the plane. When you do get to your seat, sure enough there's no place to put your bag. The hostess takes it away to put in the hold along with your supply of ibuprofen and your other flight-survival equipment. You do one last roll call; phone, wallet, passport - but you can't find your sunglasses. Then you feel annoyed, until you realise they're on the top of your head.

Once, having survived the transfer and negotiated the airport, I was sat on the correct plane congratulating myself when the baggage handlers downed tools half way through loading the plane.

I could see my bag on the wagon train through the window. But the captain saved the day; rather than miss his take-off slot, he and his crew loaded the bags themselves, much to the bemusement of the strikers, allowing us to keep our take-off slot and get away on time. I wanted to congratulate EasyJet on their captain's action but I could only find an email address for complaints.

Meanwhile you have more immediate problems because the fat bloke is spilling over the armrest on your left and the baby is screaming to your right. You smile at the baby to reassure the mother you're not having infanticidal thoughts.

The depression is more enduring than the paranoia. While waiting for the plane to take off, you start to analyse where the evening went wrong. Was it the wine, the gin, the beer, or the shots or the god-knows-what? You conclude: the blue touch-paper was lit when you picked up that very first drink and it caused the alcoholic explosion to go off. You swear you'll never drink again.

As the plane takes off, the baby screams even louder because the pressure starts hurting its ears and the child sat behind you starts his relentless campaign to kick your chair for the duration of the flight. You know there's only one way to survive the next two hours so you order yourself a double gin. You optimistically ask the hostess if she takes Swiss coins and, invariably, she will not.

The gin does its job and the depression fades. You revise your vow of complete temperance – now you'll simply never again drink the night before a flight.

Luckily, I didn't have to get up that following morning. Charlie left without me saying goodbye. I remember the transfer driver ringing the chalet bell and thinking, 'Thank God I don't have to go through GVA today,' then I rolled over and went back to sleep. The great thing about doing a full season is that you only have to retreat from the Alps once a year.

13. ANGRY PIRATES

The last time Charlie had been an Angry Pirate and finally got home he went straight to bed for a week. He was in such a state when he walked through the door that his wife almost banned him from going skiing again – well, going skiing with me at least. After considerable negotiations, Charlie had been allowed to return to Morzine if he stayed away from the rum. He returned home less hung-over and with full vision in both eyes. The bottle of Malibu remains intact to this day.

14. Piste B - Marker 7

I was looking at the face of a frightened rabbit caught in the headlamps of a car - only this rabbit was wearing a helmet and sunglasses. I couldn't see her eyes but I knew her pupils would be dilated. I knew the Ski Demons had taken over Debbie's brain from her body language.

Of all people, I should have been able to help her. I knew her history. I knew her hidden ability. I knew her emotionally. I knew her psychologically. I'd personally met most of the demons in her head. Notionally, I was even a qualified instructor.

The sun was out, the piste was empty and the snow was perfect. She knew me, she trusted me, she wanted to enjoy skiing with me, but she was struggling to act on any suggestions I made. The only smile I could extract from this rabbit was when I said, 'Okay, let's go to lunch.'

Four seasons earlier, I'd taken her and her friend down the *Coupe Du Monde* – an easy black run. There had been a few expletives but she descended it without falling. That day the only rabbit I encountered was on my plate during a rather boozy lunch. Back then, we barely knew each other; we'd met at Geneva Airport the day before. Not the romantic encounter it might sound, given she'd then had to sit in the back of Landie all the way to Morzine.

Debbie was no beginner; she'd done a lot of Wife Skiing[17] before but not always enjoyed it. Post-divorce, it was the first holiday of any kind she'd taken without her kids. A friend (Tessa) had persuaded her to give skiing another go. Now a friend of mine, Tessa will always have my gratitude – and hopefully Debbie's too.

---

17 **Wife Skiing** describes anyone (male or female) who is skiing while being shouted at by a frustrated loved one. The participants don't have to be married and the love doesn't have to be consecrated or reciprocal during the activity.

It wasn't until Debbie caught sight of one of the black piste poles that she realised she was on a black run. Perhaps I should have mentioned it - but it was no more difficult than some of the reds we'd already done.

Being with a stranger (me) she obviously didn't want to admit she was scared and neither did she feel that she could complain. With no time to anticipate, and no option but to ski the piste ahead, she just got on with the task. Her psyche was completely different.

Once romance had blossomed, she was happier to reveal her Ski Demons and probably, by confiding in me, she reinforced them to herself. I too was guilty of giving them credence. Whenever we skied together, I chose routes that avoided situations she was uncomfortable in – an increasingly difficult task. She already has the stress of commuting to the Alps every couple of weekends so I didn't want to test her love any further.

One weekend, (Season 3) Debbie agreed to ski with the newly de-radicalised David and myself. She was secure in the knowledge that there was a weaker skier coming along, who would prevent her from being T.E Charlie. By now, David had embraced the concept of 'having a nice long lunch' and the ideology known as 'being on holiday'.

Then the worst thing that can ever happen to a nervous skier, or indeed any skier, happened - she snapped her ACL.[18] Worse still, she also tore her medial meniscus, in the same knee, presumably while trying to get back up.

Interestingly, it's intermediate skiers who suffer from knee injuries the most. Their parallel-skiing technique isn't developed sufficiently to remove the danger. They use their knee ligaments

---

18 The anterior cruciate ligament (**ACL**) is a ligament in the knee. The **medial meniscus** is a semi-circular cartilage that spans the joint. The ACL can be repaired/replaced with surgery or the knee can be trained to function without it.

heavily trying to force their skis to turn quickly at slow speeds – or, sometimes, while stationary. Ligament injuries are painful and have a long recover process. I would rather break a bone than snap a tendon myself.

After an easy morning and a nice long lunch, we'd headed directly home – we were GF Skiing[19] after all. Halfway down the last blue, imaginatively called 'Piste B', David and I were given permission to sprint forward and create a bridgehead at the après bar. There was a Six Nations rugby match on and we wanted to secure seats with a view of the screen.

After waiting thirty minutes and still neither of them had appeared, I called Debbie, assuming that they couldn't find the bar. We had a confusing conversation and I was bemused that she hadn't managed to ski the last 700m without getting lost and I probably sounded a bit irritated – until she got round to telling me that she'd had a bad fall and couldn't get up.

David and I jumped back on the lift and skied down Piste B once again, looking for blood marks in the snow. We found Debbie sat under Marker 7, upset and in pain but at least there was no blood. Not really comprehending the extent of her injuries and thinking she was just being a bit pathetic, we foolishly tried to get her remounted on her skis, but to no avail. Then I offered to give her a piggyback home, but she was having none of that macho nonsense – thank God. Reluctantly, I called the piste patrol and summoned the ski-born stretcher commonly referred to as the 'blood wagon'.

---

19 Girlfriend Skiing (**GF Skiing**) involves skiing to and from lunch on blue runs with anyone (male or female) of lesser ability. No romantic connection between the participants is required.

Mercifully, I've never ridden in a blood wagon. I have however followed quite a few carrying other people during my time. The actual number I keep secret, not wanting to be tagged a Jonah. Let's just say I do it once or twice a season. I'm in no way compensated by the piste patrol for supplying customers to their lucrative trade - in fact quite the opposite. Once a guest is injured, I turn into a nurse for the rest of their stay while they sit around the chalet, moaning and demanding cups of tea all day. I don't want to sound unsympathetic but other people's injuries are a real pain for me. Once I had to carry a young lady to and from the toilet for three days – embarrassing for both of us. When she finally left, she didn't even give me a tip!

The blood wagon turned up and by this time Debbie was shivering profusely. It wasn't terribly cold so I suspected she was going into shock. The young first-aider started his diagnosis in French then reverted to perfect English when Debbie responded in Franglais.

He soon had her strapped into the wagon, Debbie protesting, 'This person is a boy; get me an adult'. The shock had seemingly turned into delirium. However, the last 700m of Piste B wasn't much of a challenge for The Boy, not even towing a fully-laden sledge. I followed carrying her skis - which was considerably more challenging for me.

Previously, while following another blood wagon down from the top of a different mountain, the piste patroller jokingly asked me which route I wanted to take, '*Shall we take zee blue or zee black?*' he enquired. To which the words, 'the fucking blue' were screamed from the sledge. That time I was carrying the casualty's snowboard and found it considerably harder than a set of skis to carry. It acted like an unwanted rudder in the high wind and I had quite a job keeping up with the wagon and avoiding the need for one myself. It didn't stop me from admiring the piste patroler's awesome snowplough. His plough could arrest the weight of two people, while travelling straight down the fall line - mine could barely slow down one.

A few minutes later, we'd reached the bottom and Debbie protested that she was a doctor and could make it home from there on her own. But anyone who gets into the sledge has to be admitted into the French medical system and needs to be signed off by a French doctor according to The Boy, so she was loaded into the waiting ambulance and off to *'zee clinique'* we went.

By the time Debbie got back to the UK, she'd racked up over £2,000 worth of expenses - the 700-metre sleigh ride had cost £350 alone. However, the real cost was to her confidence. After reconstructive surgery and months of physiotherapy, she could just walk again (without a crutch) and she'd finally got her life back – and, understandably, she was reluctant to go through the whole thing again.

Two seasons later, knee fully recovered, the more lasting psychological damage had yet to be repaired. She'd finally agreed to try skiing again, which involved not sleeping the night before we went. I too, was anxious that her return to the slopes would not be a triumphant one.

I wanted Debbie to share the joy I got from skiing. If she never skied again, she wouldn't see my favourite places in the Alps or, more importantly, visit my favourite mountain restaurants. I knew we would never ski off-piste together and we were never going to make Powder Eights together.

14. PISTE B - MARKER 7

To make Powder Eights, the first person skis down a slope leaving a perfect S-shaped track. The second person has the more difficult task and lays a second mirror version on top. They have to perfectly cross each S to turn it into an 8. Sickening – especially when they post a picture of their snowy canvas on Facebook.

Apart from the fact that I would struggle to lay the first S, Debbie had no ambition to be a Power Hound. Unlike me, there were much more important things in her life than skiing. I would always spend more time on the mountains than her, but it was important to me that we spend some time skiing together. Wherever life took me, I would always endeavour to get some skiing in every year and I wanted her to be with me each time. There was a lot at stake that day.

We had hired some short skis and set her binding ridiculously low and Debbie was wearing a custom-made brace. Her knee was perfectly safe. I'd planned the gentlest of routes that barely left the beginners area and it included lunch at *Le Vaffieu*, her favourite restaurant, as an incentive. But unfortunately the Ski Demons had won the morning session. During lunch I tried to explain to Debbie the four skiing paradoxes:

1. **The faster you go (to a point), the less likely you are to fall.**

    Explanation: the faster your skis are travelling across the snow, the more effective they become and the easier it is to control them.

2. **The faster you're going (to a point), the less falling hurts.**
   Explanation: if you fall over while travelling fast, your momentum will carry you forward and you'll slide when you hit the ground.
3. **The steeper the slope (to a point), the less falling over hurts.**
   Explanation: if the slope has a gradient, you'll have a tangential impact and your deceleration will be slower and less bruising. Compare this to falling over on the flat, where you have none of these geometric advantages and you hit the ground at a right angle and stop immediately with a thumping great whack.
4. **The steeper the slope (to a point), the easier it is to get back up.**
   Explanation: getting up is easier on a thirty-degree slope than on a ten-degree one. When you start your journey to the vertical (ninety degrees) you're already a third of the way up.

I thought they might help with her psyche and make her less afraid of going quickly or down steep-ish slopes. Embracing these paradoxes had helped me conquer my Ski Demons and they might also help Debbie defeat hers.

Despite being a scientist and understanding the geometry, she was having none of it. I told her that however nonsensical it seemed, believing in the paradoxes would help her go faster, make her turns easier and put less stress on her knee. She wasn't convinced.

I tried another approach: to make Debbie embrace more speed.

'The faster you go, not only is it easier to make turns and falling over theoretically hurts less, but you'll have to make less turns to get to the bottom of a slope. The faster you get to the bottom the more of your day you'll spend sitting on chairlifts out of harm's way enjoying the views,' I told her.

She found plenty of holes to pick in that theory too.

That afternoon, after a pleasant lunch, Debbie did ski more confidently despite her refusal to drink wine - and much faster. I like to think our little chat had done the trick, although I think it was probably the chat she had with her reflection in the toilet mirror that had been the most effective.

Piste B has taught me many lessons. Foolishly, I once jumped on the chairlift with a new guest who claimed she could ski. While ascending, we chatted and I discovered she hadn't skied for thirty years and clearly wasn't very good even then. My fears were confirmed when she promptly fell off the chairlift at the top. The whole day was devoted to getting her back down Piste B - one fall at a time. We got halfway down and even though she'd become quite an accomplished faller by then, her luck ran out at Marker 13 and her ACL snapped. She was stoic about the injury and didn't make a fuss but, unsurprisingly, didn't return to Morzine the following year. Since then, I never believe skiing self-assessments and I make sure I see people ski on a green run before I take them anywhere on a chair.

Seeing that the rabbit had turned into a bit of a hare, I though Debbie might want to lay her Piste B ghosts to rest, so I led her towards the, now infamous, run. Despite some significant improvements in her confidence and technique, Piste B proved psychologically too much and we had to turn off before reaching Marker 7. We ended up catching the Pleney Bubble down, but at least we'd done some actual skiing together and her psychological rehabilitation had begun.

Maybe I shouldn't have told her we were on Piste B, she might not have noticed and skied on. But that would have been a betrayal of trust and getting back on a horse that has thrown you, only works if you agree to get back on it yourself.

She didn't need a ski instructor to help her move her legs more effectively, but a ski psychiatrist to help her move her head. She might need someone less familiar than me to teach her, a stranger in whom she couldn't confide. Someone who didn't know her history and ability, so that she could keep her ski demons locked inside.

I once witnessed another notable knee injury on Piste B – although I'm sure they are all note-worthy for the injured. A guest once collapsed in agony while mounting his skis at the top. He rolled up his trouser leg to reveal the new location of his kneecap – it was on the side of his leg. Even now, thinking about it still makes me squirm. Some things you just can't un-see, no matter how much you try. Luckily, we were skiing with an orthopaedic surgeon. He took one look at the knee and gave it a whack with his fist and the errant cap slid back into place – another image I'll never effectively erase.

Mercifully I've never seriously hurt myself skiing - well, not on the actual slopes at least. It could be that my skiing technique is so advanced that I avoid injury. I never contort my knees so adversely that ligaments snap; I rarely fall over and when I do my falling over technique is equally advanced. Anyone who has seen me skiing will quickly dismiss this postulation. I've just been very lucky and because of the above self-congratulation, I've probably just jinxed myself.

But even though I've never ridden in a blood wagon, it doesn't mean I can't empathise with those who have and I understand that the psychological damage can be longer lasting than the physical pain. Fear of a repeat knee injury is the worst kind of Ski Demon that I've met.

Every time I ski past Marker 7, I think of Debbie and that fateful day where her confidence took a blow. It's always packed with beginners skiing erratically or blocked with ski school snakes.[20] If it's late in the day, there are also 'experts' screaming down it at high speed in a rush to get to the bar or just showing off. Late in the day, the snow is often slushy or icy and generally all mashed up. Given that everyone is tired or too relaxed and not paying attention, it's no wonder Piste B is a bad accident zone. I try and avoid the run, but it's often the only practical way home.

Just by putting her skis on and returning to the slopes, the rabbit showed great courage that day. You can only be called brave if you're first scared to death and then continue forward anyway.

---

20 Students follow their instructor in a long line with only a couple of metres between them. Often they will serpentine (**snake like**) from one side of the piste to the other making overtaking them tricky. My technique is to aim for the middle student and pass just behind him at high speed.

15. While You Were Sleeping

I'd woken up early - again. It was 5:30am and the dawn chorus was just tuning up, telling me it was summer time. The first light of morning was sliding in under a partially open window blind and illuminating the room in shades of grey. My first semi-conscious breath was of crisp clean air, telling me I had woken in a rural location. I knew I wasn't in Sutton Coldfield because the bird song was different: a cuckoo, a chaffinch and a barn owl, presumably just finishing his nightshift.

In the gap under the window blind I could see the silhouette of a train parked at a station. Slowly the light increased in magnitude and spectrum and I could see a railway line disappearing into a hill via a stone mouth to the right of my view. In fact, the track seemed to loop around me because another tunnel exit was visible to my left. Then I noticed a woman standing on the platform - perhaps she was enjoying the dawn chorus too while waiting for her train?

Then I noticed that the engine had a funnel and its carriages where emblazed with the logo L.N.E.R. and that confused me. The London North Eastern Railway stopped operating in 1903. Was I looking at a heritage steam railway or had my old friends, the Après Aliens, been messing with my space-time continuum again and deposited me in the Nineteen Hundreds? Then I realised neither was true; I had woken up in my parents' spare bedroom and was staring at my father's model railway.

The model filled half the room on waist-high trestles at the foot of the bed in front of the window so that its sleepers were level with the sleeper. I reached for the remote control - it was a hi-tech layout and steam wasn't really its driving force. I pulled the train out of the station to see if the woman would run for it but she didn't. It wouldn't be the first or the last train she would ever miss, her feet being glued to the platform. I played with the train, listening to the birds, until it was an acceptable time to get up, grateful that it was there to help me pass the dead hours.

The biggest problem with being an insomniac is the boredom. There's a reason solitary confinement is used as a punishment. There's nothing interesting to do, other than read or, in my case, write. Sartre observed that 'three o'clock is always too late or too early for anything you want to do' - existentialism and insomnia are common bedfellows.

Being awake when everyone else is asleep is frustrating. You know you need sleep and that you'll be flagging when everyone else wants to play. Being out of sync with humanity is very difficult to maintain; it's like having permanent jet-lag without the reward of exotic travel. One advantage might be that you live longer, your consciousness at least, having twice as much thinking time than normal human beings — but this is not necessarily a good thing if you're an existentialist.

The other big problem is a vicarious one. Those who choose to sleep with an insomniac (or at least next to them) can have their sleep badly affected if the sufferer doesn't develop strategies for not disturbing their bedfellow - lying very still and pretending to be asleep is hard to maintain for more than twenty minutes.

Getting up stealthily is often the solution although this takes premeditation. You have to make sure the items you need (book, laptop, phone) are to hand or findable in the dark. It's important to know where your reading glasses are, if only to establish the time. Obstacles need removing, floorboards need testing and door hinges need oiling to make an undetected escape. You then need to find a room where it's safe to turn on a lamp. It's a bit like being a burglar, although they seldom have to visit the loo en-route.

In the summer, I have the additional problem of a dog. If Oscar detects the slightest human activity he will leap into 'I want my breakfast mode' and start whining and scratching at doors. He's probably bored of the sensory deprivation too but he can't open doors or turn on lights and he's not fond of reading or writing.

Lying awake in the pitch black, with only your mind for company, can quickly lead you to ask, 'am I going insane?' Clearly something is wrong with your life and waking up early is a classic sign of depression. Maybe it's a lack of routine, a lack of physical tiredness or maybe it's just a sign that you're getting old? Which is depressing in itself. Maybe you went to bed too early? You drank too much and crashed or maybe you didn't drink enough – it's always hard getting the alcohol level right. Or maybe you're subconsciously worried about something – like not being able to sleep for instance. I take comfort in the fact that only sane people question their own sanity. Sartre suggested that 'If you're lonely when you're alone, you're in bad company.' I certainly was.

In the winter, waking up early is useful because I need to be up at least an hour before the guests. There's usually nobody else in my bedroom to disturb so if I want to engage in nocturnal activities I can. If I get up, I occasionally disturb the odd snoring asylum seeker, asleep on the lounge settees. I inadvertently wake them up when I try to do something useful with my bonus time, like unload the dishwasher – another task burglars seldom seem to do.

I generally sleep well in the Alps, probably due to my physical needs overriding the mental needs. Sometimes being asleep is the issue, with bizarre and sometimes disturbing dreams. I spent an entire season being bothered by large inflatable lobsters, although they turned out to be quite benevolent and occasionally offered me seafood. I often get cravings for seafood in the Alps, so I didn't need Sigmund Feud to help me explain it.

It seems I'm not alone in dreaming more profusely when sleeping in the Alps. Many guests claim to experience the same phenomenon. They also can have bizarre dreams, not necessarily featuring decapods.

15. WHILE YOU WERE SLEEPING

Most people put it down to cheese overdose or the altitude; but are thinner air and too much cheese really the culprits? I suspect we're not having more dreams, we're just remembering more of them.

When we go into REM sleep our brains are essentially running a defragmentation programme, ordering and storing information in deeper, more compact memory locations.[21] They pass through our unconscious consciousness. Once the 'defrag' is complete we wake up naturally and don't remember the dream. If we're inadvertently woken up and the programme is stopped half way through, our thoughts are left loitering in our conscious mind. If we drink too much alcohol, we don't bother to run the defrag programme at all and wake up less mentally refreshed - there are other physiological side effects too.

It's hard to get a good night's sleep on a chalet-based skiing holiday. Thirst wakes a lot of people. Even those who abstain from alcohol don't drink enough water during the day because the signs of dehydration are masked by the cold. Often their bodies are hurting in unfamiliar places too. Primarily, their sleep is disturbed because of those other buggers coming back from the bar so late and the bloody chalet host clattering the dishes at 7am.

There are few chalets with single rooms and most people are unused to sleeping in a room with other people who are not their spouses. Poking these people in the back and telling them to roll on their side is usually not an option. Although, I did once see one chap take a ski pole to bed. I pity those who try to sleep four-up in my

---

21 Rapid Eye Movement (**REM**) sleep is a unique phase of mammalian sleep characterized by random movement of the eyes, low muscle tone throughout the body, especially the face, and causes the propensity to dribble.

bunkroom – I often refer to the room as my walrus colony because that's what it sometimes sounds like at night.

If I've not gone skiing, I often grab a power-nap during the day when all is quiet - well, now I'm over fifty, I suppose they can just be called naps. I try not to do this when I'm skiing. It can be disconcerting waking up with a snort and finding yourself on a chairlift. It is however, encouraging that once I used to have panic attacks on chairlifts, but now I'm so relaxed about riding them I can fall asleep.

One of my guests once watched his young son disappearing into the mist on a chairlift accompanied by his ESF instructors for his early morning lesson. A few minutes later he saw them coming back down in the same chair. Something must be wrong he thought, perhaps a ski had broken or the child was unhappy. To his surprise, they rounded the lower station and went back up again. He thought the instructor must be giving his son a prolonged theory lesson. The same thing happened a further two times. Later, when he collected his son, the father asked, 'What was the instructor telling you on the first chair?' 'Nothing,' was the answer - the instructor had fallen asleep!

In my case, insomnia is a summer-only issue and is particularly annoying when you live with narcoleptics: two teenagers, a Labrador and a doctor. The teenagers, during school holidays at least, become nocturnal, and the Labrador uses sleep to kill time between walks and meals. Debbie, having endured years of sleep deprivation as a junior doctor, has the ability to sleep at will and it sometimes seems like she still hasn't caught up. (Her job still causes her sleep deprivation when she's on-call.)

If she's been operating all night, I'll often find myself in the bizarre situation where I'm eating my breakfast cereal while she's having a glass of wine before going to bed. This confuses the dog yet further and I have to play at being a burglar all day, knowing how desperate she is for sleep. 'There really is no inappropriate time to be drinking - you just need a legitimate excuse,' she tells me by way of medical advice.

If Debbie's phone goes off in the middle of the night, I'm sometimes tempted to answer it myself - especially if she's asleep and I'm awake. Having listened to her deal with calls from junior doctors so many times I feel medically trained myself.

'A-uh, a-uh, a-uh.'

'What's his BP?'

'A-uh, a-uh, a-uh.'

'What's his urinary output like?'

'A-uh, a-uh, a-uh.'

'Increase the adrenaline to 10 then call me back.'

However, I wouldn't be able to rollover and go back to sleep like she does and I certainly wouldn't be able to remember what action I'd prescribed in the morning. So far, I have resisted the temptation to answer her phone – I'd probably get her into trouble, if not kill someone.

At the weekends a teenager will occasionally move from his bed to the settee, via the fridge, and fall asleep again. This annoys Oscar who regards the sofa as his territory. Showing uncharacteristic intelligence for a Labrador, he'll steal the TV remote control in an attempt to lure the young humans off his bed. He's worked out that the TV remote is their most cherished item and often grabs it with his mouth. He can further annoy them by inadvertently changing the channel with his teeth – this is something I've been helping him work on.

I've thought about moving the settee to the garage to test the strange gravitational property it has on living flesh. But I suspect I've not discovered a new planetary force and what I'm observing is classic carnivore behaviour. When they're not hunting, eating or defending their territory, carnivores use spare time to sleep, conserving their energy for leaner times. The problem with domestic carnivores is that hunting in the fridge doesn't burn many calories and there are no lean times, because the food source magically refills itself.

Oscar, being a dog, doesn't drink much alcohol and therefore has plenty of REM sleep. It should more accurately be described as RLM (rapid leg movement) sleep. His legs twitch frenetically while he's dozing. I assume he's running after imaginary rabbits rather than from benevolent crustaceans, as in my own case. His RLM sleep is frequently disturbed - when he slides off the settee while chasing an imaginary rabbit. He then looks very confused about where it's gone. I probably have a similar look on my face when I wake up in the middle of a dream.

In the school holidays, if Debbie has pulled an all-nighter, I can be the only mammal awake all day. I sometimes feel like I'm one of those androids in science-fiction movies. I've been left to run the spaceship while the crew sleep through a small eternity in their cryogenic chambers. If I'm really bored, I'll break my programming and thaw the dog out for a walk by hoovering round his settee.

In the summer, when I do manage some REM sleep and then prematurely wake, my dreams are disturbing. They feature people and places from the past. Crimes committed and un-won arguments keep replaying. When you've spent half your adult life sleeping with one person, who is no longer next to you, it's hard not to dwell on the past. 'It's awfully easy to be hardboiled about everything during the day but at night it's another thing,' as Hemingway accurately explained.

Sometimes I think that no amount of REM sleep would be sufficient to defragment my brain. Perhaps it needs a complete reformat. A frontal lobotomy might be the answer because a bottle-in-front-of-me temporarily works.

16. The Saga Louts

One of America's greatest philosophers, Homer Simpson, once pointed out that, 'Alcohol was the cause and solution to all of life's problems,' a typically astute observation. However there's a difference between occasionally enjoying a civilised holiday binge-drink and being a drunk. Along with some of my guests, I'm in danger of becoming a Saga Lout.

A Lager Lout turns into a Saga Lout if he hasn't given up regular binge drinking by the age of fifty. By then he probably just calls it 'drinking' of course.

Saga Louts are more dangerous than younger drinkers. Not only have they had more practise but they usually have more cash. Their binge drinking sessions are not limited by funds and they can get drunk even in the most civilised and expensive bars. They're also more experienced at seeking out and consuming exotic and more potent drinks.

What most Saga Louts haven't realised is that they no longer have the immunity of youth. Society expects grownups to act grown up even when they're on holiday and Saga Louts are heavily ostracised.

Drink brings out the maverick in all of us and old people want to rebel against society almost as much as younger people. Saga Louts want to live their former life of sex, drug and rock-&-roll – or at least pretend they had that sort of life. What they don't realise is that rock-&-roll is no longer rock and roll (hip-hop has taken its place - I think), that Gaviscon and Ibuprofen are not really 'drugs' and that for 'sex' to count, someone else has to be present.

People can sometimes find it entertaining to see an inebriated youth. We recall our own youthful overindulgences and laugh. We can joke about them not being able to hold their beer then help them get to their feet. But when they see a forty-something poleaxed, they're more inclined to wag a finger and assume he/she has a 'problem' either created, or made worse by, drink.

What the accusers don't understand is that getting drunk and behaving badly is one of the last fists that can be shaken and is often our last rebellion. It's a way of proving you still exist. Remember Camus - 'I rebel, therefore I am.'

In the past, when people accused me of having a 'drinking problem', I wondered what they meant. Were they suggesting I couldn't afford the quantity I was consuming or that I was spilling too much of it on its way to my lips? Did they mean I was drunk too often or was simply drunker than them? It seemed like a very ambiguous accusation.

It is usually safe to get drunk in Morzine whatever age you are. Nobody bats an eyelid if you fall off a bar stool or start dancing like it's 1999. Unfortunately, skiing and drink aren't symbiotic despite a lot of people thinking that they are. Skiing can cure a hangover but a hangover can't cure your skiing problems. In fact, it usually makes them worse.

It's always a nightmare on the slopes, if you're leading those who have over-indulged. Simply keeping them all together and successfully getting them home becomes a challenge. Saga Louts on tour are the worst of all.

Towards the end of Season 6, I broke my golden rule and agreed to take ten chaps from Hull round the PdS circuit, an easy if long, route to ski. Ten exceeded the golden rule of keeping skiing groups down to eight. Eight is a 'stable octet' and above that number there are usually free radicals trying to break free.

16. THE SAGA LOUTS

Clearly some of the chaps were suffering from the excesses of the night before, but I stuck to my plan and, after cracking the whip a couple of times, I got them half way round. We then stopped for lunch in my favourite restaurant in *Châtel* (*Le Vieux Four*). Wine, beer, and a complementary *digestif* were consumed with *verve*.

Lunch had dragged on and we were a little short of time if we were to catch the critical last lift out of *Plaine Dranse* and avoid an expensive taxi ride home.[22] When it came to leaving I noticed that some of them were having problems mounting their skis. This was alarming because we had a long way to ski home and some of them were not only drunk, but tired. I returned to being their taskmaster and we cracked on. In my rush, I lost two of them en route.

They'd skied down a right fork, having not listened to my instructions nor seen me ski down the left fork. I kicked myself for not labouring my instructions nor shouting them out. I hadn't made eye contact with all ten of them before setting off either, to see if they were paying attention. I hadn't stopped at the beginning of the fork, instead I'd skied out of sight round the first bend - I'd broken all the leading rules. I had to make a brutal call: did I accept my losses and get the remaining eight home or mount a search party and potentially lose even more people? I decided on the former and accepted I'd failed as a guide.

The remaining eight were ecstatic when we finally got back to Morzine and après commenced. I don't think any of them had skied so far in a single day before and, for some of them, in their entire lives. Several admitted to having had feelings hate towards me half way home – but that's all part of being a ski-host. The lost two turned up after (impressively) finding their own way home, much to my relief.

---

22 In the Alps, it's often faster to ski to a destination than drive. The skier can take the direct route, over the mountains, while the driver has to take the meandering roads around them. And, in the case of a taxi driver, it means charging an enormous fee to cover the return trip.

A rather glamorous and drunk Canadian girl, not quite yet a Saga Loutress but on her way, decided to join us, or rather she fell off her skis into our table. She was a WAG of one of Morzine's ice-hockey stars; she'd been trapped by love in Morzine, where all there was to do, according to her, was 'frigging ski and frigging drink' - which pretty much sums up life in the Alps.

The biggest problems with being a Saga Lout is not losing your faculties but losing your property. When the Après Aliens conducted their abduction campaign on me, they seemed to like collecting souvenirs. Often it was a hat, a glove or a pair of sunglasses but occasionally my wallet, my phone, or my keys would go missing. This could just have been a function of old age and an ill-advised purchase of a coat with self-emptying pockets. I got to the stage where I was reluctant to take anything important out with me if I knew I was likely to get drunk. I felt that, like a soldier going into battle, I needed to leave all my personal effects at home in case I was caught, frisked and interrogated.

Drunk or sober, your possessions are often in extreme jeopardy in a crowded après bar. People shed their clothing like Russian dolls when they enter the bar straight from the piste. Coats, jumpers, helmets, rucksacks and a plethora of other items needed for skiing, end up in piles all over the place. And many people own the same brands, models and the same size items - skiers often look like clones after all.

Saga Louts, in particular, have a habit of accidentally taking home the wrong coat, which is a disaster if it's your coat — especially if your phone or ski-pass is in it. The trick is never to leave anything important in your coat and to sit on it, just to make sure. There's a lot to be said for wearing an appallingly loud, ugly or unfashionable jacket that no else would be seen dead in – or at least that's my excuse.

I've lost count of the number of times I've had to retrace the previous evening's itinerary with a guest, trying to reassemble their belongings. Saga Louts can be like small children, leaving a breadcrumb trail of discarded clothing behind them. I go with them for moral support and in some cases because they don't know exactly which bars they were in. I quite enjoy watching them sheepishly revisiting the scenes of their crimes. Each bar will probably have a pile of around a dozen items left behind from the previous night.

I'm also amazed at the number of items people leave in the chalet. My lost property box (well, it's more of a sack) is always overflowing with ski clothes, goggles, sunglasses and shoes, by the end of the season. I take the sack back to the UK and try to reunite the items with their rightful owners – well, if they don't fit me, I do. Once, I even found a sex toy (I think) left in one of the rooms! I really didn't know how or where to start to reunite it with its owner. On the whole, most things that remain unclaimed end up in the charity shop – but not the sex toy for obvious reasons.

My other problem with feckless Saga Louts is that they often take my stuff, mistaking it for their own. Important cables, chargers and power adaptors are all on my 'at risk' list, along with the ski-passes, socks, hats and gloves I've lent out. Importantly, my drugs (Gaviscon and Ibuprofen) also go missing. Most of my medical kit, along with my toiletries, ends up back in the UK before I do.

You don't have to be a pensioner to be a Saga Lout; you just have to be old enough to know better but not care what other people think of you (even if you do). I've discovered that doing things considered tragic for a forty-year-old can actually make you endearing when you're fifty. At fifty you enter a category called 'there's life in the old dog yet' and become admired for still being 'with it' by mimicking youth or trying to relive your own. This is why I always smile whenever I see a Grey on a Tray,[23] but this doesn't seem to apply to deliberately getting drunk.

I'm not sure if there's a generation gap anymore. I used to dress, act and think very differently to my folks but now the generations overlap in music, morality and fashion. We all wear T-shirts, trainers and jeans; we all communicate using texts - I'm not sure why they're called phones anymore because few of us use them for speech.

Perhaps I'm unaware of the gap because I live in a middle-class world. The kids I know don't skip school, binge-drink or take drugs. They don't smoke and seemingly can't even be bothered to get pregnant. Their politics are more right wing than they should be too. I know your socialist brain cells are supposed to die first but they should still be in the majority when you're eighteen.

The problem with the-kids-of-today is they show too much respect. Frankly they're the most boring generation yet. Crucially, they're happy to live with their parents —why would you leave a free five-star hotel when the management are so cool? Perhaps parents have cheated modern youth out of their rebellion by being so rebellious themselves. Sartre's opinion on the matter was, 'I hate the crimes of the new generation: they are dry and sterile'. Unfortunately, he was talking about *my* generation – maybe it was different in France.

Saga Louts often become philosophers while propping up the bar. They have more experience, albeit clouded, of life. They often come to some amazing conclusions that I feel I should write down in my phone - assuming I've not lost it. I look at these notes in

---

23 A **Grey on a Try** is an old snowboarder who often has, but not necessarily, grey hair.

the morning and can never remember why I found the sentences I entered so profound - assuming I can decode them.

Existentially speaking, we are all free to drink whatever and whenever we like. Existentialists don't judge themselves using the morality of others. Saga Louts have simply taken Descartes slogan and given it a twist of lemon - 'I drink therefore I am.' But them, alcoholics have clever ways to justify their drinking.

When people accused me of being an alcoholic, what did they mean? That they saw me drunk too often? Or just that they were soberer than me? Did they think I was damaging my life or having too much fun? I may have misread the odd situation as to how much fun I was supposed to be having but, if I did have a drinking problem, it was the problem of choosing where, when and with whom I got drunk; that's where I went wrong.

You don't have to be an alcoholic, unhappy or bitter about life to behave like a Saga Lout; you sometimes just get sucked in. The drunken bravado and good humour at the bar makes you forget you're no longer young and you assume you'll be forgiven if you behave like an ass. That's when you start drinking wine in volumes that should be reserved for beer and you find yourself shaking a fist at age and dancing to songs from another era.

It's always best to refer to Hemingway for definitions, especially when it comes to drink. He observed that, 'alcoholics don't drink to get drunk, they drink to stay drunk'. That counted me out; I always sobered up for long periods in between. If I 'drank to forget', it must have worked, because I can't really remember why I did it so much. I mostly drank because it was fun - until it wasn't so much fun anymore.

17. Failed Domestic Goddess

When I was a younger man and an even bigger idiot, I used to think being a housewife was a cushy number. My only excuse was that I'd been brought up with the male thinking in Yorkshire at the time. Back then, most families had two parents (one of each) and there were few working mothers, like my own, pioneering the feminist cause.

Seeing a working mother at close range, through a child's eyes, it didn't seem that big a deal to me and I presumed that other mothers who didn't have an actual job must be slackers. I didn't really know what being a housewife involved, both physically and mentally, just that it meant staying at home all day, apparently doing whatever you liked – it sounded good to me.

I now know it's a tough job with long hours and a seven-day working week. It requires knowledge, discipline, dedication, and advanced logistical skills and, most of all, mental self-sufficiency. Sometimes, it's like being Robinson Crusoe.[24]

Despite the skills needed, it attracts little appreciation and is not given enough respect as a profession. In traditional Jewish grandma (bubbe) thinking, wanting to be a housewife was a noble ambition.

The career path involves starting out as a trophy wife by finding an upwardly mobile husband (a doctor is ideal). Then you have kids, with the prospect of living a life of leisure once they've left home – occasionally doing some consultancy by interfering in their lives. Even if your husband went trophy hunting again, you

---

24 The fictional character, **Robinson Crusoe**, fled Britain after killing a friend over love. He then gets shipwrecked and had to fend for himself on an uncharted island. He saves, and befriends a native he calls Friday (novel written by Daniel Defoe in 1719).

ended up with half a luxury life and the kids looked after you when you got old - that is the theory.

My own Bubbe, being more enlightened, didn't give my sister that advice and probably never thought about suggesting housewifery as a career for me. Although if she could have seen ahead, she would have pointed out that I'd forgotten to marry the Doctor, the kids weren't mine and neither were half of the luxuries. And if I was indeed a mere trophy husband, I was one without tenure nor indeed the looks.

Post mid-life crisis, it might have looked to the uninformed observer like I had a cushy summer life as a househusband. But, three summers on, all was not well in Sutton Coldfield. Initially I had taken pride in my new work and wanted to be a domestic goddess. My primary objective was to make the breadwinner's life pleasant and relaxing when she got home. However, there were three powerful Agents of Entropy (two school kids and a dog) tirelessly working against me.

Being a goddess was tougher than I thought. It wasn't just about being a good cook and preparing interesting and healthy meals; I thought I did a pretty good job of that in the chalet, although the few vegetarians who've stayed with me might not agree. In Sutton Coldfield, I soon discovered that feeding vegetable phobic people was harder than feeding vegans - if you cared about their health.

If you want to gain goddess status, you need to implement and ruthlessly maintain a zero-tolerance cleaning and tidying regime. Chalet Neige had a cleanliness rating of four out of five on Trip Advisor. I was quite proud of it, until it was pointed out that most of my reviewers were blokes – apparently we use a different scale to women when rating cleanliness.

To get the goddess badge you also need to be the master of laundry. School uniform items must move instantly from the bedroom floor and magically appear, clean and ironed, in the wardrobe. In the chalet, people are mostly responsible for their own clothes. Although I have observed many mothers who need the laundry lullaby syndrome - they can only fall asleep if they can hear a washing machine or tumble dryer running in the background.

Then there are the administrative tasks I didn't realise a domestic goddess has to perform: the organisation of the social diary, the planning of holidays and making sure the endless bills get paid. Like most good personal assistants, I made lots of lists (or was given them) of jobs that needed doing.

You're either a list person or you're not. For me, the only thing that surpasses the pleasure of writing a 'to-do list' is striking an item off it once the task's been done. Sometimes I start the list with things I've already done, then immediately strike them through. Admittedly, quite a lot of the items on my lists get transferred to the next day's list. I run two lists: the 'WIP List' (Work In Progress) and the 'IG List' (Instant Gratification) so there's always something to strike out.

Although it's not strictly a core requirement for passing the 'Domestic Goddess Test', being good at DIY can score you bonus points. Just as they did in the chalet, the Agents of Entropy worked tirelessly at the fabric of the house and things just fell apart on their own. Not a week went by in the summer without me having to fix something - mostly toilet seats. Mainstream goddesses are allowed to use the GSI option (Get Someone In), but since I was striving to be a masculine goddess I needed to strap on the tool belt myself.

There were some readers who lambasted *Skiing with Demons* as a misogynistic work, but if they'd really digested its contents they would have realised that it's actually an assault on the male stereotype. The truth is, I'm an emancipated man and I'm happy to do 'women's work' – whoops.

17. FAILED DOMESTIC GODDESS

After three summer seasons of trying to be a domestic goddess, I decided I was a lost cause. I decided the petty battles with the Agents could not be won. I grew tired of trying to provide acceptable yet healthy food and my cleaning standards dropped.

I knew when they'd fallen below an acceptable level because Debbie started using phrases that she thought I might relate to: 'Can you do a full chalet changeover tomorrow?' or 'Is it time for an end-of-season deep-clean?'

Paranoia set in and I started to suspect that my new family were taking in laundry because they surely couldn't be getting through that many clothes on their own. I even thought about making the Agents wait outside the house until the evening inspection had been done.

I knew I'd lost the desire to be a domestic goddess when I found myself in Asda buying pre-chopped vegetables and a jar of Dolmio™ meatball sauce. I realised I'd turned into a slummy daddy when, at the checkout, I looked down and noticed my jogging bottoms were filthy and saw my slippers poking out beneath them.

Fortunately, being a good househusband is not just about being a domestic goddess it also involves being a good listener.

In the evenings, house cleaned, washing done, dinner ready, dog walked, token DIY task completed, properly dressed and with my makeup on, I listen for the bread winner's car to arrive. I try and greet Debbie by the front door with a glass of wine in one hand and *her* slippers in the other – that's if I can find where the dog has hidden them. I then ask the important question, 'So darling, how was your day?' The answer to which goes over my head. Apart from the technical jargon, I initially found the politics in the NHS impenetrable, although, after three years, I think I've got a good grasp of what ails the organisation – too many sick people and not enough doctors. Then, out of politeness, she asks how my day has gone. However, after hearing how her latest lung transplant went, I don't feel much like telling her about the great achievement of my day – alphabetically arranging the spice rack.

Often the worker has been talking all day and simply wants to sleep. Some days the most intelligent life form I've spoken to is the dog (my Man Friday) and he's not much of a talker - thank heavens for Facebook and Mumsnet.

Being a househusband involves more than just listening; it involves being understanding and soothing the worker's troubled brow. It involves subduing your own petty problems – the worker doesn't want to hear about self-invented First World problems or your existential angst.

I now know it's not so easy being a housewife and why so many become neurotic about cleaning and some even write 'Bloody Books'. I also know it's not easy for an existentialist to live with someone with such an altruistic career as a doctor's - when your business is saving lives you don't have to look very far to see meaning in your own.

I'm often embarrassed for Debbie when her doctor friends ask what her partner does. She must be at a loss to describe it. She could lie and go with, 'He retired early,' intimating some illustrious career and a fortune sitting in an offshore bank; or she could go with 'fingers in pies'. They don't need to know she's mostly referring to the crusted kind. Now I'm an existentialist, I care less what people think. If I find meaning and purpose in my life, it's no less valid than the meaning and purpose of others. I usually go with 'Trophy Husband' myself – and wait for their reaction after they've looked me up and down. Now I've written two books I might start using 'author,' although I suspect that will attract similar smirks. As every unheard-of actor knows - you have to suffer for your art.[25]

I'm envious of Debbie's impressive and meaningful job, if not her brutal schedule - she is my trophy wife not I her trophy husband. By comparison, being a housewife *is* an easy job - but it's hard spending your summer days marooned on a domestic island.

Anyway - a *man's* work is never done, so I'd better stop writing and get on with the housework because the Doctor and the domestic Agents of Entropy will soon be home – I think we'll have meatballs for tea.

---

[25] Sartre tells us that, 'All human actions are equivalent and all are on principle doomed to failure.'

18. Powder Demons

Despite having been declared a 'good skier' (whatever that means) by the Ski Club of Great Britain, I knew I was a fraud. I still struggled to ski well in deep powder, especially in the proximity of trees. Even though I made out that I was a powder hound, I was just going along with my peers. I was supposed to be a powder-seeking missile, intent on making fresh tracks. To be a truly complete skier, I had to get the powder demons off my back.

It seemed to be the ultimate goal for every skier: to bounce down through a forest in waist-deep powder with a quirky high-tempo sound track running through your head, if not actually coming in through your ears – possibly 'Jackson' by Johnny Cash.[26]

We have Warren Miller to thank for this. His ski movies have set the inspirational agenda for decades and consequently made everyone else feel like bad skiers. When I watch a Miller movie or the ubiquitous screens showing epic powder descents in après bars, I too want to be a ski movie star.

Most skiers of my age will have watched *The Blizzard of AAHHH's*, a movie made in 1988 by Greg Stump that often gets the accolade 'the best ski movie of all time' - which is a little short-sighted. It's about the history of extreme skiing and features rebel skier Glen Plake with his trademark blond Mohawk hairstyle. It has a typically West Coast sentiment and is a little dated now. It's also a history lesson about ski fashion. It still entertains

---

26 Obviously, I never listen to music while skiing – that would be distracting and irresponsible. And Johnny wasn't singing about Jackson Hole nor, as far as I'm aware, ever went skiing.

if only to see what passed as skiing fashion back then, including helmet cameras the size of breeze blocks. Warren Miller, now retired, made more photographically stunning films with more up-to-date technology and slightly less insane ski stars than Greg Stump and perhaps that's why he's the chief culprit.

I'd listen to other self-declared powder hounds talking a good game in the bar. I'd occasionally ask them what exactly they did differently with their legs in powder to avoid the trees successfully. I started to suspect most of them were frauds too.

Everyone had a top-tip, mostly to lean back or put your legs closer together, but I couldn't find that one enlightened individual who could give me one killer piece of advice on how to ski powder. I was looking for a magic bullet but I'd collected a magazine's worth of blanks.

Being a bad workman I blamed my tools. I started to think that maybe I had the wrong skis. Powder hounds like to bang on about ski technology, using terms such as 'width under the foot', 'rocker', 'side-cut' and 'flex'. I wasn't entirely sure I knew what they meant. They usually had some radical planks themselves in which they had total faith. They would sling them over their shoulder after giving me the benefit of their wisdom and stride off like a movie star. Often, I'd catch sight of them skiing very badly down a red run the next day.

We all tend to buy skis for the skiing we dream about doing, not the skiing we actually do. Assuming you only have one set of skis, which most recreational skiers do, you need a more all-mountain ski. Most people spend eighty percent of their skiing time on-piste and only five of the remaining twenty percent off-piste in powder. Having said that, when the surf is up. 'You've got to be ready to catch the wave, man' - I'm practising my dialogue in case Warren calls.

Initially, I went searching for a pair of magic powder bullets. I tried just about every type of ski in Michel's shop. One of the great things about running a chalet is the relationship you develop with a ski hire shop and those who work there. Not only do the ski dudes working at Gravier's give me some genuine 'powder houndly' advice, I can also borrow just about any ski they have.

I settled on some twin tips. Not because I wanted to ski backwards or do tricks in the park, but because they suited my laidback skiing style. Leaning back instead of correctly leaning forward, like most folks, was my biggest problem. This, however, exacerbated the real problem - I wasn't actually a very good piste skier. I still had elements of rotation in my turns especially if I was nervous and trying to rush them, which I invariably did on steeps and deeps. On-piste my skis were generally above the snow and this didn't matter so much, but when they were under the snow, any attempt to rotate a ski would trip me up.

I realised that all those instructors were right; I needed to become a better piste skier in order to conquer the powder. I needed to perfect the carve-turn on-piste; I needed to use the shape of my ski to steer, without any lateral involvement from my knees at all. If I did the same in powder, and forgot about controlling my speed, it would work there too. Of course, I had to discuss this with the Ski Demons first. They begrudgingly allowed me to give it a go on gentle powder slopes.

I discovered that if I pointed my skis down the slope, once I was going fast enough, they would rise above the snow and their behaviour would become more familiar. It was the same revelation I'd had when learning to ski on-piste – speed was, and had always been, my friend.

Once I just tried to steer rather than slow down, I discovered that the speed was self-regulating. Like the bow wave of a boat, the snow I was displacing would check my acceleration. I just needed to hang on for the ride until terminal velocity was reached, then start the turn. The terrain would set that terminal velocity; I just needed to choose the steepness of the slopes I attempted and the angle at which I attacked them. It seemed to work. If I had a wide enough canvas and used a large font, I could draw big S shapes down the fall line.

This however was not the full solution. It wouldn't allow me to ski powder through trees, unless they were fifty metres apart, and that couldn't be classified as skiing in trees - that was skiing *near* trees not in them. But at least I'd moved on to the next level. If, by mistake, I found myself in the woods, I'd revert to my trusted TRC methodology. To ski powder in trees properly (whatever that meant), I needed to master the short linked powder turn.

The key to making short linked turns is rhythm. The timing and placement of your pole plant that starts each turn is critical. Unfortunately, I was not blessed with rhythm – those who've seen me dance will testify to this. Humming to a tune with a beat helps. I usually choose something between AC/DC and Leonard Cohen depending on how short I want the turn to be. When I see others doing short turns I wonder what song they're humming in their heads.

I wasn't very good at short linked turns on-piste. After a few turns my arms get out of sync with my legs and I'm planting my left pole somewhere behind me when I should be planting the right one in front. 'They look like the lips of an actor in a badly dubbed film,' as one instructor described it. I set about improving my short turns on-piste and have yet to master them - I haven't quite found the right tune.

Perhaps wanting to ski fluently through dense forests in deep powder, was asking too much. Was it far too ambitious for an old ski-dog to learn one last new trick? Was it even worth him trying? Had he reached his skiing equilibrium - where the pain didn't justify the gain? I knew I'd never get that call from Warren, unless he decides to make a special film called *Geriatric on Skis*.

However, like most skiers, I'm the star of the ski movie I'm making in my head. I visualise the last sequence – I'm weaving through the trees, powder flying everywhere, looking like a needle dragging a thread. I haven't chosen the sound track yet.

19. The Soggy Bottom Boys

I've never tried snowboarding, therefore my opinions on its merits are invalid. However, they're no more invalid than those of a snowboarder who's never skied. It doesn't stop some of them from offering their opinions, so I'm going to offer mine.

I'm probably too scared to try boarding now and not because I'd probably injure myself - although that would be a concern. No, it's because I've invested too much time, effort and pain into becoming a good skier (whatever that means) and I'd be foolish to even try. Having finally started to see a return on my investment I'm reluctant to switch codes.

Most boarders are equally entrenched in their discipline so objectivity is hard to find – but it's always fun to talk about something you don't really understand (like existentialism) so here goes. I may not have experienced the joys of boarding but I've observed the problems encountered when trying to move around a snow-covered mountain on a tea tray - and some of the advantages too.

If I did decide to become less bigoted and strap my feet to one plank instead of two, the marmite problem would resurface and there would be one of two ultimate outcomes.

1. I'd hate it. This is the most likely outcome. I'd get frustrated and demoralised with all the things I got frustrated and demoralised with when learning to ski. A whole new set of neuroses would develop and the Boarding Demons would be born. The only upside would be that I'd probably get enough material for a third book.
2. I'd love it. If I discovered that I was a gifted snowboarder – unlikely, I know - and that snowboarding is a lot more fun than skiing, I'd be equally demoralised and frustrated

that I'd wasted so much time on skis. I'd also be forced to eat my beanie hat having made so many jokes about boarders in my time.

If 2 were the outcome, I'd have to change more than my mode of transport. I'd have to learn a new language if I wanted to hang with my boarding bros – and we've already established how good I am at languages. I'd also have to make decisions on which way to ride: goofy, regular or duck-footed and I have no idea what those words mean.

I'd have to change my wardrobe too. I'd be very self-conscious having to wear a lurid jacket and trousers two sizes too big. I'm a fan of loose-fitting clothes and have recently discovered the joys of elastic waistbands, however I don't want to look like I've inherited my big brother's ski gear or stolen my son's. I may have had a self-confessed midlife crisis but I don't want to walk around advertising the fact.

Snowboard boots look more comfortable than the torture devices we skiers have to wear. They look easier to get on than ski boots but smell more when taken off - well, they do if you use a skier's nose. They tell me ski boots are not supposed to hurt when you're actually skiing, so I must be doing it wrong. I often think the most pleasurable part of skiing is when I take mine off - if I took up boarding I'd have to forgo that joy.

I'd have to change my music too, which I'm not prepared to do. It's apparently important to have some 'banging beats to get me pumped, so I can ride like a pro.' (I have no idea what I just said, but I already feel cooler).

Snowboarding music has its origins in the West Coast grunge culture that just about made it into my musical consciousness – if owning one Nirvana CD counts. But soon after I bought it I reached my musical death-age (45) and my ears became closed to new music.

19. THE SOGGY BOTTOM BOYS

I remember my musical death. My car radio inexplicably tuned itself from Radio 1 to Radio 4. Frankly it was a relief. Trying to recognize new artists to prove I wasn't old was becoming an onerous task. Once you reach your musical death-age you can just say, 'fuck it, I've always liked country music,' and you no longer need to listen to Johnny Cash in secret. After your musical death you can concentrate on rediscovering the music from your own youth and fill your iPod with tracks from back catalogues. Anyway, back to snowboarding.

I'll accept that snowboarding is cooler than skiing, but is it easier? The circumstantial evidence suggests it is. It's got to be easier to control one item of equipment than four, if you count a skier's poles. There's a lot less things to get tangled up, tripped over and impaled on. Also, keeping your centre of gravity above two edges has got to be harder than above one, especially if the edges can move apart. Most humans, however, find it more natural to have their feet pointing in the direction they travel – only crabs move sideways.

Learning to snowboard from scratch looks like very hard physical work. I can see it takes more core strength to repeatedly get into the crab position and then stand up without the help of poles.

Most of your first lesson will be spent flip-flopping around on the ground. From a distance a class of beginner boarders can look like a pod of beached seals. At least a beginner skier can listen to his instructor while they're both standing still. Being able to move your legs independently, however encumbered, means you're not rendered entirely immobile on your very first day.

Once you've mastered the basics of boarding, it becomes easier to become proficient. There are no intermediary steps, such as snow ploughing and step turns, to be learnt and then unlearnt on the way.

On a board, falling over in powder doesn't involve the arduous recollection and reattachment of equipment. Getting going again after a fall seems a simpler task. In fact, a good boarder (whatever that means) can disguise a fall as a trick if he returns to the crab position in one continuous move.

Skis have a habit of falling out with each other, ejecting their owner and going their separate ways. A board is more faithful and will never leave its owner and hide somewhere under the snow.

It's definitely harder to move around a ski resort on a board. Most resorts were designed for skiers, before boarding was invented, and have very boarder-unfriendly infrastructure. Chairlift designers assumed passengers would have both their feet pointing forward and this makes disembarkation tricky for boarders. The designers didn't visualise anyone ever wanting to go sideways on a draglift either, making them a nemesis for many boarders.

Then there are the flat bits to negotiate. You need more gravitational assistance to make a board move forward than you do with skis. That's why boarders regard any slope less than 10% as flat. Luckily, boarders wear comfy boots and so walking across the flat bits is no big deal. Unfortunately, this means they have to detach one leg from the tea tray and walk like a human with an enormous clubfoot. This 'clipping in' and 'clipping out' of their bindings before and after every chairlift (and flat bit) is very time consuming. For most boarders, fiddling with their bindings means sitting down in the snow so acquiring a permanently soggy bottom and a greater risk of haemorrhoids. Skiers can traverse genuine flat bits using relatively humanoid leg movements (shuffling or skating) without having to sit down and get a cold and wet bottom first.

19. THE SOGGY BOTTOM BOYS

When I have the privilege of leading boarders around the PdS, many accuse me of taking boarder-unfriendly routes. Some think I'm doing it deliberately to prove the superiority of my skis, but I'm not. I understand their special needs but it's hard to avoid flat bits and draglifts in any resort. Some suggest the PdS isn't a very boarder-friendly area, and then it's me who protests. 'All *ski* resorts are unfriendly to boarders,' I tell them. 'The clue is in the name.'

There's no getting away from the fact that skis are better all-round tools for dealing with difficult terrain. Skis generate less friction and consequently need less gravity to help make them slide. They're therefore faster downhill and glide further across flat bits. They have more edges to grip icy slopes and are more effective for making an emergency stop.

There's also a variety of ways to use skis should you find yourself in a tight situation and can't make a turn. A good boarder can of course descend without turning and can move backwards much more easily. Skiers can remain stationary while they work out what to do – this is not always a good thing.

A family that regularly stays with me consists of three generations of boarders: grandfather (seventy-ish), his son (forty-ish) and his three teenage grandsons. I've had the privilege of leading this boarding dynasty around the PdS. When I come to a stop, they all sit around my feet making me look like a zookeeper about to feed his seals. We usually have a few sporting gibes about the merits of skiing versus boarding. The great thing is Grandpa is the best boarder – although he used to be a skier, which, I joke, is why he's the best. I call him a grey-on-a-tray and he calls me a skinhead on skis. The truth is I admire him taking up snowboarding at the age of sixty – something I'm not be prepared to do at fifty.

Ski historians will point out that modern carving skis evolved from snowboard technology and the skis we use off-piste now, especially the twin-tipped ones, look like snowboards and work very similarly – we keep them close together and are effectively snowboarding, just with our body and feet pointing forward.

Boarding is evolving too. I had one snowboarding pioneer stay with me who'd cut his snowboard down the middle to get over the perambulation problem when he wanted to go over flat bits or indeed uphill. He had a bolting system to make them one unit for his descents. These are becoming more popular and are imaginatively called 'split boards'. I call them skis.

Perhaps the most interesting question is: would a caveman choose to ride or glide? We know that skis were used as transport over 10,000 years ago thanks to a cave painting found in China – unless of course the Chinese of that era had extremely long feet. Even though animal fur was still fashionable and Kurt Cobain had yet to walk the Earth, I suspect that if we put a snowboard in front of a troglodyte's cave his children would soon want to ride it.

Some skiers feel boarders are less in control. I've noticed that if there's an unfortunate collision between the two different codes, each will assume it's the others fault. When describing an accident, skiers will always make a note that it was a *boarder* that cut them up and boarders will always emphasise that it was a *skier* that caused the collision. We all seem to remember the idiot's mode of transport rather than the idiot himself.

Learners of any type are dangerous but the boarding demographic is skewed towards the young and reckless. There's a Highway Code of sorts (the FIS Code of Conduct[27]), which lists ten basic safety rules, but nobody takes a theory test before going out on the slippery white roads. Perhaps resorts should make it compulsory before handing over a ski pass or at least insist on new skiers and boarders alike wearing 'L' plates?

I had my own nasty incident with a youth (who coincidentally was on a board). I'd just passed the slow-down sign at the entrance to a village where I intended to take my group for lunch. I broke my rhythmical turns and headed towards the restaurant's ski rack. The boarder, going much faster, presumably to minimise his walk to the lift ahead, tried to overtake in the dwindling space between the rack and myself, a space that soon became non-existent. He spectacularly splattered into the rack ejecting skis in every direction much to the amusement of those dining alfresco.

Trying not to laugh myself, I asked him if he was okay. This was misinterpreted as an admission of guilt rather than simply a concern for another human being – you have to assume people are human in the first instance. He responded with a torrent of abuse. My response was to quote the FIS code using my best schoolteacher's sarcasm. 'You were overtaking me. I don't have eyes in the back of my head. Did you miss the large orange sign in the middle of the piste that said 'SLOW' in three different languages?'

The rest of his non-secular tribe arrived dismounted and squared up to my group, who were a collection of middle-aged ladies. The previous day, I'd been leading the ten burly blokes from Hull, which, initially, I thought would have made a fairer fight, but I was wrong. My ladies were armed with pointy sticks and enough attitude that the boarders beat a hasty retreat – the

---

27 **FIS**, short for *Fédération Internationale de Ski*, is the world's highest governing body for international winter sports. Responsible for the Olympic disciplines of Alpine skiing, cross-country skiing, ski jumping, Nordic combined, freestyle skiing and snowboarding.

protagonist shoulder-barging me on the way past in a final defiant gesture, while telling me, 'I'm not a fucking skier, so the code doesn't apply to me!'

I'm not entirely safe myself. Once while trying to impress Debbie by skiing backwards, I crashed into a toddler. Fortunately, she wasn't harmed, just a bit frightened, as was I when her dad skied over. I apologised profusely in my best Franglais, I picked her up to demonstrate she was fine but she burst into tears with a 'Make the nasty man go away' look on her face. Dad mustn't have seen my orientation on impact but I got away with it un-chastised.

Well, not entirely. 'I know you don't like kids, Chris,' Debbie said later, 'but there's no need to mow them down.'

Boarders always complain about groups of skiers blocking the brows before hidden drops - I hate this too. Skiers do it, subconsciously or otherwise, so they can assess the drop or gather their energy before embarking down it. They may be doing it to make sure there isn't a line of boarders sitting below the brow – something skiers often complain about. Boarders do this, subconsciously or otherwise, because it is easier to sit and then get back up on a slope than on the flat brow. Of course, both are breaking an FIS golden rule – you should only stop at the side of a piste.

Another common accusation skiers have for boarders is the unpredictability of their trajectory. Skiers theoretically indicate, with a pole plant, which way they're about to turn. When overtaking a boarder, you don't really know which way they might turn next. Maybe other boarders can tell from body signals that skiers are unaware of? Having said that, my pole plants are a bit random and I'm not entirely sure which way I'm going to turn after making one myself.

The Ski Nazis, also like to stoke the boarder versus skier animosity, if only in jest. They have a larger investment in skiing than me and therefore have an even more deeply entrenched and uninformed opinion.

One day I found myself skiing off-piste with the Ski Nazis and a soggy bottomed boy called Shahbaz. Unexpectedly we found ourselves skiing through some trees. David decided to headbutt one of them. I'm not sure what it had done to annoy him, but he then fell into the trench around its trunk.[28] David got stuck upside down in the trench with his legs waving in the air.

In hysterics, Val and I reached for our cameras but Shahbaz realised that David was actually suffocating under the snow. He lay down on his board, grabbed David's legs and pulled him out. David emerged with a bloody and unamused face. He was angry at the paparazzi for taking pictures instead of mounting an immediate rescue. Now, whenever he japes about boarders, we remind him that one once saved his life.

Unbelievably there are still resorts in the USA with a boarding ban. If their intention is to keep out the disrespectful, inconsiderate and rebellious youth they will fail. The generation that pioneered boarding has grown up and made boarding mainstream. If a youth today wants to rebel against the older generation, he'll probably don a pair of skis.

Being a newly born existentialist, I now refuse to belong to any one school of thought. Boarders and skiers are both making pointless journeys through hazardous terrain in a paradoxical and

---

28 Pine trees melt six inches of snow around their base creating a **trench,** which can be more hazardous than the tree itself. Other hazards include stumps left by felling activity, low hanging branches and other skiers who have stopped for a tinkle.

irrational universe. If an individual finds purpose in his journey, it's irrelevant if they use one plank or two. I accept other people make different choices in music, attire and life and I respect other people's freedom to choose boarding – so long as they know and abide by the FIS rules.

20. The Book Run

Four years in the living and three years in the writing, 'The Bloody Book I' (SWD-I) was finished. It was finally for sale on Amazon - and 'other reputable outlets'.

However, if I wanted people other than my friends and family to read it, the real work, the marketing, had to be done. Having worked in the industry for most of my latter years, I should have been good at that. At least this time I'd be promoting a product I believed in – almost.

It was rather ironic that the Chalet Project, which was supposed to prevent me from having to do, or ever use, the 'M word' again, was forcing me out of retirement. I'd like to tell you that I'd spotted a gap in the publishing market and deliberately crafted a book to fill it – but I didn't. I wrote the only book I could write and luckily it was rather, for the want of a better word, 'unique'.

There were biographies of famous skiers and lots about skiing itself, but none about a rubbish skier who got drunk a lot. There were plenty of books by those whose mountain adventures were more radical than mine, but none were set in Morzine. There were some written by pioneering ski instructors, but none who lived in Sutton Coldfield.

Luckily, I hadn't forgotten all my online marketing skills and once again I set about deploying a social media campaign. Thanks to four years of running the Project, I already had reasonably large social networks (both on and offline). I thought most of my previous guests would buy it, if only to check if they needed the services of defamation lawyer – no chance; I'd taken an editorial decision to say only nice things about people – other than myself.

If you say or write bad things about people, the reader thinks bad things about you. If you say good things about people, they think good things about you – or so the theory goes. Some people think it best to dance round the truth and let people read between the lines – but not if they are from Yorkshire. After reading SWD-I, most people thought good and bad things about me in equal measure – it's a bit of a Marmite book. Perhaps that's the mark of a good author – his books should taste of Marmite?

On publication, there was an initial surge in sales, which I put down to family, friends and guests, and then there was a worrying pause. Perhaps I'd not been revealing enough. I started to regret not calling it 'Fifty Shades of Snow' and removing the salacious content the early draft contained.

My next bit of good luck happened when the Daily Telegraph reviewed the book and branded me a sexist - you can't buy publicity like that. Sales from unknown people started to mount. Proving that having bad things said about you, makes people think you're good.

My real break came when someone started a discussion on snowHeads[29] about SWD-I and I realised where my true audience lay: middle aged folk who love skiing and hate their jobs – which is most of them. I was living their dream or at least had been foolish enough to try.

Thanks to all that serendipity, SWD-I was an Amazon best seller over Christmas and ended up in many skier's stockings. Offline sales, however, were tiny. A few people were ordering it from bookstores but I'd yet to have the joy of walking into one

---

[29] **snowHeads** is an online forum for all things skiing related and quite a lot of things that are not.

20. THE BOOK RUN

and seeing it on a shelf. I knew my main chance for doing that would come in Morzine. I had to get a season's worth of stock (an unknown quantity) to Morzine before the season started and convince some local retailers to put it on their shelves.

Debbie and I departed for Season 6 carrying more books than bacon, turning the Bacon Run into the Book Run. Landie axles strained under the load - a hundred copies of my life were a very heavy burden.

Landie mostly behaved herself, despite the extra load. She did break down ten metres from Debbie's front door, which with hindsight was very considerate. It was the fuel pump again – the fourth I'd replaced on Trigger's Broom in as many years.

It's always an emotional departure, leaving the people you love, but I knew many of them would visit me in the Alps. There's an element of dread, that life will once again become gritty and you'll not always have a proper bed. However, the overall feeling is of happiness that summer is over and you're returning to doing what you love best. Any existentialist angst would be buried deep below the snow and the real problems of day-to-day living in the Alps. Surviving and prospering were reasons enough to live. Even if some of the challenges were self-made, like skiing down a steep slope, achieving them seems to give life a purpose. And of course, looking at those all-important views makes you feel privileged to be alive.

We got to Morzine the night before I took over the chalet and we checked into Le Dahu, one of Morzine's more upmarket hotels. I pretended this was a reward for Debbie's endurance, having survived her third bacon (now book) run. But it was really a last treat for myself before starting my Spartan winter life.

A mythical mountain creature, the Dahu, is a goat-like animal that has legs on one side shorter than the other. This enables it to stand on steep slopes. However, it must also mean it can only travel in one direction. From my research, it's unclear if the left or right side legs are shorter. This leads me to think there might be left-footed and right-footed subspecies, which brings up some interesting Darwinian problems. If lefties mate with righties would their offspring lose their lop-sided advantage? Then I realised that cross mating wouldn't be possible because animals from different subspecies would only be able to approach each other head on.

Once I'd settled into the chalet, I started my door-to-door book salesman's routine. I've never found cold-calling easy and hate it when salesmen knock on mine. It was excruciatingly embarrassing for me because I was selling something so personal and I had little evidence that it wasn't junk.

My most difficult challenge was to persuade the bookshop owner in Morzine to stock SWD-I. I should really have taken a translator because his Frenglish was worse than my Franglais. I had to explain the contents of the book through the medium of mime. He was obviously impressed with my acting or simply wanted the English loony out of his shop, so he bought ten copies. They sold quickly and he restocked. He then put a copy in his window and his shop became my best outlet. I suspect he still has no idea what the book is about - come to that, neither have I.

I also plastered Landie with posters and parked her in the centre of town. Congratulatory messages were left under her wipers, the first one of which I initially mistook for a parking ticket.

My other tactic was to use pretty girls. Marketing isn't really that difficult, especially in 'Manzine'.[30] Willing female friends would

---

30 In January, Morzine is often referred to as '**Manzine**' because the town becomes flooded with men. The ratio of men to women is especially high in January because low season prices and reliable snow attract men on their annual boys' skiing trip.

sit in a bar then start talking about the book to the suitors they'd inevitably attract. Then the author (me) would coincidentally materialise with signed copies under his arm.

Michel my friend, and owner of Gravier's ski shop was an early adopter and refused to take any commission. His generosity to my guests and myself has always warmed me. He once joked, *'If ze customers break a leg, I only charge zem for the renting of one ski.'* The truth is he doesn't charge them at all.

He's always got an amusing story about his life and the people who frequent his shop. He should write a book himself although, when considering some of his adventures, it might be better published posthumously.

Most people who stayed in the chalet bought a copy of SWD-I, presumably out of politeness, but I think it helped that I left a copy under everyone's pillow. It may have helped some of them get to sleep.

I had a lot of help with my sales and marketing strategy from a chalet chain owner (Stuart). I think he empathised with my narrative and found my observations accurate. Perhaps my experiences were not so unique and they'd just never been documented.

One of my most successful outlets was a restaurant called Le Clin d'Oeil, a favourite of mine. The owner and two of the waitresses, both from Transylvania, had read and, surprisingly, enjoyed the book; I was amazed that they understood my British humour. The owner, Kristel, kindly displayed the book on her bar and my Transylvanian fan club (I've always wanted one of those) enthused about the book to their slightly pissed diners. Kristel refused to take any commission although I did spend much of my newly gained literary fortune on her superb cassoulet.

I was told writing a book was the easy bit. Now I can confirm the more difficult task is getting people to buy it. However, Landie returned from Morzine that season with an equally heavy load, but most of the books had turned into wine - the 'wine run' was still the 'wine run'.

The reviews started to mount up on Amazon and mostly they were good. There were a couple of people who hated it and felt the need to tell me so while hiding behind anonymity. I might have written a Marmite book, but at least it wasn't bland.

If you did buy a copy in Morzine, I'd like to thank you, and for reading this one too. You might have wondered why the book smelt of bacon with a hint of diesel fumes – well now you know why.

21. Boyfriend Skiing

I refer to it as 'Boyfriend Skiing', or BF skiing for short, but any romantic connection between the participants is optional. It describes the common problems faced by women who are significantly better skiers than their hairier halves.

Theoretically, thanks to EasyJet, skiing is now a pastime that transcends class. It may now be more affordable, but it wasn't always so. Being a good skier is often a sign of a privileged upbringing. If your parents were reasonably wealthy, you might have been skiing since you were a child, but your BF might not have been so privileged. It's always tricky falling in love with someone from the other side of the tracks and skiing can expose the divide.

Or your BF might be the heir to a fortune and simply rubbish at skiing. He may have come to skiing late or be fonder of eating cakes. He may be older and less athletic or he may simply be scared of heights – there's always an acceptable excuse and it's best to acknowledge it.

The most common problem for both parties is recognizing that they're in a BF skiing relationship. Men always think they're better skiers than they actually are, and most women underestimate themselves. Girls, if the skills gap is unarguably in your favour, you may need to manage the situation carefully.

If he's a beginner, it's not a good idea to dump him in ski school every day while you bugger off into the backcountry with Jean-Pierre, a local guide and notorious Lothario. And even if you're a qualified instructor, it's a worse idea to try and teach him yourself. If the skiing relationship is to survive, you'll need to spend at least one day BF skiing with your beau, if you want to regularly winter holiday with him again.

BF skiing means adopting the same attitude needed for successful Girlfriend Skiing. It means waking up on the designated

BF day and saying to yourself - 'today I'm Boyfriend Skiing' then flicking your boots into walk mode, grabbing some short thin piste skis and taking your camera instead of your transceiver.

Meanwhile the BF will be having a team chat with his reflection in the bathroom mirror. 'Today we're going to leave it all on the mountain; don't let her see your fear.' 'Move aside, Jean-Pierre, I'm taking my woman back.'

However, BF skiing is harder to pull off than GF skiing thanks to the fragile nature of the male ego with the additional complication that most men don't like being told what to do. Most also have a sexist opinion of female navigational skills, so, girls - you've got your work cut out.

There's an art to being in control without looking like a control freak, which must be mastered before attempting BF skiing - the passive-aggressive approach works well. 'Where would you like to ski today, darling?' you ask, while having your own plan perfectly formed. Whatever he comes up with first, just say, 'well that's fine, it's your day dear, wherever you want to go, we'll go.' Let him cycle through alternatives until he hits on your plan, then agree it's the best option.

Before setting off, run through a full equipment check – remember he's just a large child and you're simply taking over from his mum. Always make sure he's applied sunscreen to his face. He might not care about his skin but if his skiing improves sufficiently, making marriage a possibility, you'll be looking at his mug for a long time.

If he isn't a total beginner, the choice of terrain is critical for a successful day's BF skiing. Try to find empty wide blue runs to allow him to ski at ludicrously high speeds without endangering others and always ski behind him yourself. Expert BF skiers can occasionally request he slows down. Stroke his ego by telling him that you can't keep up, not that you're worried about his safety.

If he has a spectacular wipe out, after checking there is no real injury, give him time to dust himself off. If he blames his bindings, show concern and don't point out that in certain situations skis are meant to fall off. Don't give him advice on how to remount his skis more effectively. He may be biding time and waiting for the pain to subside or the dent in his ego to smooth itself out. If he's taken a whack in the gentleman area, it's always best not to laugh.

If he insists on returning to the ski shop to get 'better skis' or more wax, just wink at the shop assistant and he'll know to find something more appropriate than the monsters your BF originally chose.

There's a right way and a wrong way to hire skis. BFs often choose the wrong way if they're trying to impress someone such as their girlfriend.

The ski dude, who works in the shop, will usually ask some questions to make sure you get the right skis and more importantly set your binding correctly. He needs to establish, weight and height and, most importantly, your ability.

Your height is fairly obvious and an experienced operative can measure it with his eye. However, guessing someone's weight is a delicate business and he may keep that assessment to himself. If he does ask your weight it's best not to lie. Whatever you tell him, he'll assume you've lied and factor in a correction – usually half a stone.

Then he'll enquire into your ability. He may have made an initial assessment the moment you walked in the shop. By judging your deportment, clothes and the way you describe the skis you want, he'll already have a good idea of your ability. But good skiers come in all shapes, ages and sizes, so he'll usually ask.

He might simply ask, 'How many weeks have you been skiing?' and work it out from that. He's assuming, not altogether accurately, that people improve each year. If he asks the question directly, 'So, how good a skier, are you?' You must choose your words carefully and even better, have them rehearsed, if you don't want beginner's skis or a pair of suicide planks.

You need to come up with some words that will convey your ability while maintaining an air of modesty. Before I had my own skis and took responsibility for my own binding settings, I used to say, 'Not as good as I should be, considering how many weeks I've skied,' and force a little laugh.

Once I accompanied a seventeen-year-old into Gravier's and she got this horribly wrong. When asked the dreaded question she simply said 'expert'. The ski dude (Pete) gave me a knowing glance then set her bindings for an intermediate skier who still had a lot to learn.

If you think your BF is able, it's always good to find an easy black run that he can notch up on his belt and give him something to brag about in the bar later. Avoid all mogul fields, couloirs and heavily wooded areas – they'll expose his lack of turning ability. You might get a free helicopter ride out of it, but you're the one who'll be helping him to the toilet for the rest of the week.

The choice of lunchtime restaurant is also important. It must have a swanky wine list enabling the BF to show his superior expertise in something. Don't worry, he'll usually choose the second cheapest bottle. For similar reasons, allow him to order his own food in French and don't laugh when the snail consommé turns up. Also, remember to be impressed when he, inevitably, wants to show you the top speed of the morning that he recorded on his skiing app.

Sartre's girlfriend, Simone de Beauvoir, took him BF skiing in Chamonix in 1934. Beauvoir was also an existentialist writer, political activist, feminist and social theorist. Of course, simply calling her Sartre's girlfriend really does her an injustice and she would probably have balked at the term. In her book, *The Second Sex*, she points out that skiing is a great gender equalizer: 'The featherweight boxing champion is as much a champion as is the heavyweight; the woman skiing champion is not the inferior of the faster male champion'. We've already heard Sartre's own views on skiing. It must have been fun listening to them bicker on the chairlifts – assuming you could understand the French. When I hear a French couple having a heated conversation on a chairlift, I assume they're discussing where to have lunch, not philosophy.

After lunch it's especially important to keep the BF away from ski-school areas. Most men suffer with PLAD (post luncheon attention deficit) and he'll ski like a missile with faulty guidance software. If he does take out a kindergarten class, ski past until you're out of sight then wait until the shouting dies down.

Remember, despite the picturesque scenery, the log cabin accommodation and cosy blazing fire, it will be wise not to expect romance in the evening. You may be on a holiday but he's on a survival course - so don't wear him out in bed.

If none of the above appeals, you may be better suggesting that your boyfriend tries boarding instead. This will give him a world of his own to master. If you're truly committed to the relationship you could level the playing field by learning boarding together. This would have the added benefit of annoying your bigoted skiing dad, who won't like the prospect of having a boarder for a son-in-law and even less for a daughter. Given all the money he spent on your skiing lessons, it may cause him to despair – unless of course he's an existentialist.

I do believe it is possible for mixed ability couples to enjoy a skiing holiday equally together, but only if the better skier understands the principles of Boyfriend Skiing or indeed Girlfriend Skiing. Interestingly, which approach will be most effective with your worse half, isn't always determined by their sex.

22. Chalet Raspberry & The Cresta Run

At the end of Season 5, I closed the front door of Chalet Neige not knowing it would be for the last time and that the Chalet Project would soon be in crisis. I'd packed my worldly items into Landie and completed the deep clean. I'd dropped the shutters, putting the chalet to sleep and assumed I'd be back after my own summer hibernation.

The owner rang me a few weeks later and told me the bad news. Thanks to his own impending divorce, Chalet Neige was up for sale and I wouldn't be able to renew the lease. I empathised with his plight, having travelled down that dimly lit road myself. Even if I'd wanted to, there was no way I could afford to buy the chalet.

It was devastating news. At the time, I was unaware of the works of Sartre and had yet to become an existentialist - I decided to end the Project and do something *others* would find acceptable with my life.

After a few months of sleepless hibernating in my *cave-de-homme* (man cave) I woke up. I looked out of the window at the suburban abyss known as Wylde Green and panicked. I began to search the internet for another chalet, although it was almost August and I'd probably left it too late. I had to put the metaphoric band back together, get the show back on the road and rehearse some songs - time was short.

On the recommendation of a friend (Liz), who was still on the ground in Morzine, I booked Chalet Framboise totally unseen. It was some distance up the *Vallée de la Manche*, an area I didn't know very well. It was a bit of risk - no, it was a hell of a risk for an unlucky person. The chalet had a raft of operational uncertainties: how well equipped was it, was it accessible on foot, was the freezer big enough for my bacon cache? And, most importantly, was the garage habitable?

I didn't really know anything for certain, other than that the chalet had a silly name. I knew Framboise was French for raspberry but not that raspberry implied 'fruity' in a gay sort of way. I took the fun name as a good sign. At least it was catchier than *Chalet Neige* (chalet snow) and it appealed to what was left of my marketing brain.

I'd seen pictures of the chalet and a floor plan online, so I had some idea of its decor and layout assuming that the marketing material could be trusted. The website, like any such material, only described the chalet's virtues. It failed to mention that it was up a steep and narrow access road, soon to be christened the 'Cresta Run' or that it was in an avalanche-risk zone – and there was no mention of the resident evil cat.

When I first stepped inside Framboise and saw the view from the window, I knew I'd made a good choice; trees, mountains and even a babbling brook could be seen. If it's *raison d'être* was to improve the view from my window, then the Chalet Project had been given a new lease of life.

A beautifully converted farm building, Framboise had far more character and old-world charm than Chalet Neige. It made you feel that you were truly high in the Alps, something that wasn't always obvious at Chalet Neige, which was surrounded by modern, if traditionally constructed, buildings.

Framboise was bereft of many of the problems I'd lived with at Chalet Neige that had been getting on my nerves. It was more luxuriously appointed and, critically, the double beds could all be split into twins favoured by my predominantly single guests. I was pleased to discover the kitchen had a six-ring gas hob. I'd come to hate the tiny electric cooker at Chalet Neige. I never thought I'd have a preference or indeed get so excited about kitchen appliances – or turn into the discerning chef I had apparently become.

Having leased Framboise via an agency, they were responsible for cleaning and doing the dreaded changeovers, which was a real bonus – hearing that I wasn't going to be responsible for laundry was music to my ears. Making sure there was always enough linen, of the correct quantity and size, had taken advanced planning skills – a headache that would now belong to someone else.

When I first arrived, I discovered Framboise was a *very* safe distance from the Buddha Bar. A lot safer than I'd been led to believe. In fact, there wasn't a bar of any kind within practical staggering distance. I knew this was going to worry some of my diehard après-going guests. I would try and encourage them to eat and drink in the chalet, which would boost my profits or at least cover my increased rent.

I knew a very different type of season was afoot. At least the Après Aliens wouldn't be able to find me - unfortunately neither could most of my guests.

When I first approached the chalet I noticed an avalanche alarm on the side of the road. Given the history I've shared with that particularly powerful Agent of Entropy, I was concerned. The alarm consisted of a large yellow sign that had a rotating red light on top. Translated, the sign said, 'When the red light flashes, wait until it stops flashing.'

I was reassured when the owner told me there hadn't been an avalanche in the valley for over sixteen years. He also assured me that the Crêt, immediately above Framboise, protected it. [31] The main avalanche danger was round the corner where the buildings were not in its lee nor that of any other reliably immovable barrier.

Having just met the owner, I didn't know much about him. I didn't know if he was a theist, a fatalist or simply a scientist putting his trust in a large mound of earth? I wasn't sure, although

---

31 A **Crêt** is a common Alpine name for a lump of rock or earth that is bigger than a mound and smaller than a hill. The number of French words for 'hills' is almost equivalent to the number that Eskimos have for snow.

I was reassured by the certainty of his beliefs when I found out he lived next door.

Later, while exploring the hamlet, I found a memorial plaque next to a Catholic shrine. It commemorated a farmer's wife who saved her family a century or so before. One New Year's Eve, she had a very bad feeling and made her family move out for the night. She implored her neighbours to do the same and she must have been quite a sales woman because they all did. An avalanche did indeed descend that night but, thanks to her, only property not life was lost. Nowadays, electric sensors at the top of the mountain set off the avalanche alarm – we no longer have to rely on the bladders of old women for early warning systems. Anyway, back to the present.

The owner went on to tell me about the various granite boulders that seemed randomly scattered around the place. They too periodically tumble down the mountains clearing all in their path. Some had made nice garden features and some more recent additions had come to rest inches from front doors.

We all have to be philosophical about the things life throws at us. However, living in the mountains can literally mean not knowing who or what may soon come knocking on your door.

Above Framboise the one-track access road continued, clinging onto the side of the mountain. It had a rudimentarily safety barrier to prevent vehicles falling twenty metres onto the main valley road below. The barrier leant out twenty degrees above the vertical and was covered in paint marks, which suggested it had been extensively tested. The road then crossed the avalanche zone, squeezed through two old wooden buildings and looped back onto the main road below.

The managing agent's website had mentioned that snow chains *might* be necessary to access the chalet, but I then had to discover for myself how difficult getting a long-wheel-based vehicle in and out of Framboise's parking space actually was. It involved a very tight turn off the access road, narrowly missing the neighbour's overhanging eave.

I tried approaching the chalet from above and below. The only practical solution was to drive up the hill and straight into the space. This meant that on departure, I had to reverse onto the lane, stop, execute a hill-start then continue up round the ledge, across the avalanche schuss, wiggling through the wooden buildings (taking care to avoid hooking Landie's roof rack on their low-hanging eaves) and back down onto the main road. All reasonably achievable when the road was dry, but not so easy when it was covered in snow or, worse still, in ice.

Unfortunately, my first week in Framboise had some unseasonably warm weather and a repetitive freeze-thaw cycle turned the access road into my very own Cresta Run.

Landie is best when the snow is deep. Its thin knobbly tyres soon find grip and with the diff-lock engaged it can climb seemingly impossible slopes. However, on icy roads it handles like any two-ton vehicle, possibly worse. Add the weight of eight people and the driver starts to feel like the captain of an oil tanker, planning changes of course several miles in advance.

It took me a few weeks to work out the best strategy for accessing the chalet. Returning to the chalet was easy in any conditions although it took commitment. I simply had to turn of the main road at full speed - or as fast as I dared. Momentum would then take me up to the chalet and, in one smooth move,

I'd turn into the parking bay, making sure I didn't rearrange the neighbour's guttering en route. However, if I anticipated ice in the morning I'd approach from the top and reverse in so I could exit down the slope in the morning and avoid the hill start. I soon realised that snow chains were essential most of the time.

One morning, after a starry and chilly night, I congratulated myself on successfully orientating Landie the previous night in the right direction for a descent. Everyone got in the back bringing the axle load up to around four tons. I started down the Cresta Run then noticed that pressing the brake pedal had no effect. This became more concerning when I realised that no matter who had the right of way, I was going to join the main road without stopping. Luckily no cars were coming and once the rear wheels hit the dry main road we stopped.

While re-establishing my breathing, I heard a loud car horn and looked up and down the road but it was clear. Then in my mirror, I saw another vehicle coming down the Cresta Run with its driver gesticulating wildly through the windscreen - presumably having problems braking too. Then I realised, there was some bloody idiot blocking his exit – me. I slammed Landie into gear and with my wheels spinning and just got out of the way as he schussed passed my tow bar.

I learnt many lessons in alpine driving that winter. The most important of all was that, if you're thinking of putting your snow chains on, you probably should. Although having too much confidence in chains was almost my downfall once.

On another icy day, I'd approached the chalet from the top and stopped outside the chalet. I was only popping in to retrieve something I'd forgotten, so I left Landie running in neutral on the road with the handbrake on. I'd forgotten that I only had chains on the front wheels and more importantly that the handbrake only locks the rear ones.

While walking round the back of the vehicle I leant on the rear door to prevent myself slipping on the ice and Landie move forward. Nudged by me, she had started a pilotless descent of the Cresta Run dragging her rear wheels behind her. I scrambled round the moving vehicle, dived into the driver's foot well and pressed the footbrake with my hands. This applied the front brakes and the chains gripped and we eventually stopped.

I don't know if anyone observed my predicament. If they had, it would have given them a good laugh. It must have looked like some crazy English fool was trying to drive his Land Rover while standing on his head. My troubles weren't over. Next, I was presented with my own amusement – how to replace my hands with a foot without releasing pressure on the pedal. By the time I'd solved this contortionist's conundrum, I'd complete forgotten what I'd returned to the chalet for – but another lesson was learnt.

Slowly, I found ways to make Chalet Framboise work. That first month of Season 6 was very stressful. Dealing with the Cresta Run wasn't my only problem and the Agents of Entropy were rife. I was very disorientated and disorganised and kept losing and breaking things – Landie broke down twice.

One big problem with Framboise was that the garage was not habitable and I ended up sleeping in the laundry on an air bed most nights. Initially I missed my garage in Chalet Neige, which was luxurious by comparison. At least the laundry was safer – it didn't have an exterior door that jokers could use to insert horses and I couldn't accidentally press a button in my pocket to remove a wall and freeze myself to death.

Unfortunately, in the laundry the soil pipe near my pillow gurgled every time someone flushed the loo leaving me with unsavoury thoughts about what was passing inches from my head.

I had intended to be peripatetic, utilising any room or bed that wasn't occupied depending on the sleeping requirements of the guests. But not having any permanent place to keep my things meant that I was always losing stuff. If you've ever lived out of a suitcase for three months, you'll know how mentally stressful not having a permanent camp is.

I didn't realise how important knowing which side of the bed your phone will be in the morning was and which side to get out of in the night without bumping your head. If you don't know where the light switch is or the direction of the toilet door, you can often find yourself lowering your shorts while stepping into a wardrobe. Also, if you change rooms too often, you run the risk of accidentally climbing into someone else's bed, which can often be misinterpreted – or so I found.

Once things settled down I got myself organised, established a routine and started to enjoy the Chalet Framboise experience. On the whole it was better than Chalet Neige. I enjoyed exploring the *Vallée de la Manche* and discovered a new side of Morzine, one that I ended up loving the most.

Some of the Project's regulars thought so too and embraced the change. However, the single diehard après goers found the location unworkable not being a staggering distance from town.

Despite the problems, I signed up for a 2nd season in Chalet Raspberry, even though I knew I'd lose the patronage of my favourite cougars and wondered if some of my manthers would ever return. The Project had started a new era and I had a new winter home more suited to my existential needs.

23. Le Chat Noir

Season 6 got off to a very stressful start. I only arrived a couple of hours before my inaugural guests and I had to hit the ground running. When they arrived, they kept asking me where everything was and how things worked – questions I couldn't answer because I didn't know myself.

That first night I had to perform the ultimate in stressful tasks: I had to cook dinner in a stranger's kitchen – but at least I was 'cooking with gas'. While trying to find the correct utensils, at the correct time, I was inundated with requests for piste maps, lift passes, hairdryers, power adapters and, of course, the WiFi code.

Before smartphones, only a small group of addicts would rush off an aeroplane and stampede outside to light a fag. Now there's a medley of pings when a plane lands because everyone needs to check that their online world was not destroyed while they were in the air. On arrival at the chalet, polite guests will wait a respectable amount of time before asking me for the WiFi code – which is between thirty and forty-five minutes. Most youths will ask for the code while walking through the front door - I think it's their way of saying hello. I like to mess with their heads and tell them the router is broken. Anyway, dinner is ready.

Despite not being able to locate anything quickly, dinner was a success and the guests were finally subdued and lying sozzled on the settees in the living area. But my work was not yet done; there was still the small matter of the washing up.

It was cold outside and mercifully the rain had turned to snow. The guests had finally shown some initiative and worked out how to start a fire in the log burner all on their own. They'd put a sizable forest into it and turned the chalet into a sauna.

Still grafting in the kitchen, I'd got a bit of a sweat on. In an attempt to cool off, I opened the VELUX roof window above the sink - once I'd found the opening pole. I inadvertently pulled the window past the horizontal and all the snow slid off it onto my head, which instantly cooled me down.

Refreshed, I returned the window to forty-five degrees (almost-closed), swept up the snow and returned to the washing up. I could hear the eerie noise of the wind gusting outside, interspersed with the crackles from the fire and the belly laughs of my merry guests, who had now moved on to the brandy. Then I heard a faint but plaintive cry.

I looked up and saw two green marbles with elliptical black centres staring at me through the gap in the window. They made me jump and I dropped the pan I was drying onto the draining board. This made the apparition jump too and it fell through the gap and landed on the work surface like – well, like a cat.

More of a kitten than a cat, it was skinny, but it had a black velvet coat. Once it regained its composure by pretending it had jumped not fallen, it started licking leftover butter from one of the plates and purring. It was rather cute - apart from its evil eyes.

Most people in Britain regard black cats as omens of *good* fortune. I'm pretty sure in Yorkshire we regarded them as *bad* luck - but then we think most things are. The Scots in particular believe that the arrival of a black cat to a home signifies prosperity. However, in Western history in general, black cats have mostly been looked upon as a symbol of evil, being the witches' pet of choice. So most of Europe considers black cats as *bad* luck, especially if one crosses your path, which is believed to be an omen of death. I was unsure if falling out of a window in front of me counted as 'crossing my path' and I thought nothing more of it.

I went to stroke the intruder but it scampered off into the living area and introduced itself to the invited guests, with mixed reactions. People often declare themselves to be either cat or dog people and personally I prefer the loyal stupidity of a dog to the manipulative intelligence of a cat. But although I'm a dog-lover, historically, I've borne cats no ill.

That was about to change.

Le Chat Noir, as I imaginatively named him, was clearly a frequent visitor to the chalet. He strutted around like he owned the place, jumping from lap to lap until he found the biggest cat-lover in the building. Unlike dogs, cats can tell where their best interest lies. I left my guests arguing whether to give him a saucer of milk or throw him back out into the snow and I went to bed.

The following morning, I was up before the guests to prepare breakfast. While cooking the eggs, I noticed *Le Chat Noir* helping himself to a croissant from my pastry basket. I batted him off it and rearranged the basket so the nibbled pastry was hidden. He'd obviously won the vote on his eviction and had been locked in the chalet all night. After breakfast, using milk as a lure, I caught him and put him outside before leaving the chalet myself.

I returned to find the bloody thing back in my kitchen, this time licking the chicken I'd left out to defrost. He had obviously found another way in because the roof window was firmly closed and more snow had covered the glass - resetting the booby trap.

This was the start of my battle to keep the *Le Chat Noir* out of the chalet. Each evening before going to bed, I would check the perimeter, closing window and doors, but somehow the cat always found a way in. At one stage I thought there must be an unknown breach in the chalet's perimeter or that he snuck in through windows opened by guests in the middle of the night. But all he really had to do was bleat at the balcony door and some cat-lover would take pity.

A few days after the black cat had 'crossed my path', the inaugural guests left, I went to the supermarket, while the cleaners prepared the chalet for my next group. It wasn't long before I got a call from their boss - someone had apparently been sick in their bedroom and left it as a parting gift. I got a lecture about acceptable behaviour and how it wasn't their job to clear up sick. Mortified, I assured them that I now attracted clientele who seldom vomited or would at least clear up their own sick if they did. After a lengthy investigation, including some forensic analysis, *Le Chat Noir* got the blame – it was cat sick.

After sick-gate, exhausted, I retired early that night to my laundry. I flopped on my airbed but it was deflated and my bones impacted with the tiled floor. *Le Chat Noir* had been in and punctured it. Luckily I had a spare – well, it wasn't luck, just good contingency planning.

Being an unlucky person, I have a spare one of everything. Whenever I leave for a season I always ask myself the what-if questions: 'what if I lose my phone?', 'what if my credit card gets stolen?', 'what if I lose my key?' and 'what if my airbed gets punctured?'. I make sure I have a backup plan, which usually means having two of everything and, importantly, keeping them in different locations.

The next set of guests, a bunch of chaps on a work-organised trip, arrived. After a predictably large first night, I took them to the ski lift in the morning, some looking decidedly pale. I returned to

23. LE CHAT NOIR

find a scene of unimaginable horror - a pool of diarrhoea all over one of their beds. It had soaked right through to the quilt. Initially I suspected one of the guests, but after an awkward conversation, I realised it was that bloody cat again. Obviously, butter, croissant and raw chicken hadn't agreed with him. The previously white bedding must have been the closest thing he could find to his normal latrine – the snow. Luckily I had a spare quilt and bedding.

The rest of that January was marred with disasters. Some were directly attributable to *Le Chat Noir*. He punctured my spare airbed within a week of the first and continued to leave me 'presents' whenever he got locked in.

Some disasters were not obviously the cat's fault. But, every time I saw *Le Chat Noir* something bad would invariably happen: the coffee machine exploded, the washing machine leaked, important charging cables broke, things went missing. Morzine Mary actually broke her leg, the day after stroking the cat. But rather than blame misfortune, bad planning, or poor decision-making or just general clumsiness, I blamed the cat. I'd become a superstitious person, most unlike my old self.

I've never counted magpies or thrown spilt salt over my shoulder. I don't walk under ladders, but only because that's where paint often falls. I'll open an umbrella in a house if there's a leak in the roof, and cross people on the stairs if there's room. I'm completely happy riding on a chair if it's numbered thirteen. I don't have a lucky rabbit's foot nor a special pair of underpants. Instead, I carry pessimism with me and it works like a charm. But now I had come to believe in the evil power of a black cat whose sole purpose was to make my life hell - I was clearly losing my mind.

I used to be a man of science, before existentialism came my way. I thought everything could be explained with maths, physics and chemistry and if it couldn't, natural forces as yet undiscovered were probably at play. But no matter how large a view we have of a picture, the reason it was painted will always be impossible for science to explain. The cause-and-effect thinking of a scientist doesn't have a start or an end; he/she can only explain the things in between. So, I've stopped looking for answers in science and started blaming cats instead.

One morning, I noticed that *Le Chat Noir* hadn't joined us for breakfast and I assumed for once that the perimeter had held. Pleased, I went about my morning routine - getting the guests dressed, fed and out of the chalet as quickly as possible.

Leaving the more organised to correctly dress themselves, I went out to warm up Landie - she is one old girl that can't be rushed in the morning. *Le Chat Noir* was sitting on her bonnet and giving me the old evil eye.

After I'd excavated Landie from the overnight snow, I jumped in and turned the key – but she wouldn't start. I tried all my usual tricks to get her engine running but nothing worked. When the battery was finally flat, I looked out of the window in despair and saw the cat sat on a nearby windowsill. He appeared to be grinning. It was at that point that I realised that *Le Chat Noir* wasn't simply a harbinger of bad luck; he was a powerful Agent of Entropy and I'd underestimated my foe.

In desperation, I asked my neighbours if *Le Chat Noir* belonged to any of them, but I was told he was a free spirit and that they too occasionally fed him. I felt like asking if they had bad luck but thought better of it. Nobody claimed ownership of the wretched animal. I'd forgotten that, unlike dogs, cats choose their owners rather than the other way round and, clearly, *Le Chat Noir* had chosen me.

Then one day he vanished. I assumed he'd chosen another owner or that my nightly border patrols had finally started to work.

Despite our differences, I really hoped that he'd not had a bit of bad luck himself and been run over. However, immediately my luck started changing. Things started to run smoothly at Chalet Framboise - frankly there was nothing much left to go wrong. Then, several weeks later, he crossed my path for what would be the last time.

I was heading to the UK for a mid-season break and while sat outside the chalet, waiting for my transfer to the airport, he nonchalantly strolled passed looking very fat. He clocked me sitting on the doorstep and came bounding over.

We greeted each other like old adversaries - he jumped on my lap, started purring and I rubbed his chin. While doing so I wondered if this meeting meant my plane would crash. It didn't.

After I returned to Morzine, the cleaner gave me an update - our working relationship had improved since sick-gate. She'd found *Le Chat Noir* in another chalet about to give birth – it turns out he was actually a she (remember, I told you I wasn't cat person). I hadn't seen any other cats around that season and wondered where, in the bleak midwinter, a cat went to get laid – possibly the Buddha Bar, I thought.

I never saw *Le Chat Noir* again but now, whenever I see a black cat, I shudder, fearing that it may be one of her offspring.

24. One Flew Over Laax

Zurich airport was crowded. I jostled for a good position behind the arrivals barrier holding up my sign. It said 'Hello I'm Vanessa', which clearly wasn't true. There wasn't space on the paper to explain why a bald and bearded man was calling himself Vanessa and I was getting some funny looks. The real Vanessa had been unavoidably detained and I was her substitute.

When the Ski Club asked me to help lead their over-fifties holiday in Laax, I immediately said yes, even though I had no idea where Laax was - I'd never even heard of it! It had been a year since I'd qualified and I was keen to see if my blue jacket still fitted. I wasn't sure why they'd asked me, having no knowledge of Laax to offer, but I was grateful to be given the opportunity to wear my jacket in action given the trouble I'd been through to get it.

Perhaps they though my efforts needed rewarding, or that, because I was over fifty myself, I would make a suitable ski-host. There would be another experienced Leader (the real Vanessa) on the trip too, so I assumed I would simply be a back-marker and would be learning the ropes from her. I was wrong.

I'd applied for leading slots in all the places where I could claim to have some knowledge of the terrain, but most of them were in France. The Club had suspended leading in France the year I qualified – just typical of my luck. [32] I looked Laax up on the map. It was in the German-speaking canton of Graubünden on the north-east side of Switzerland, near Lichtenstein. It was a tiny ski resort, with very little terrain to worry me – or so I thought.

I often ski from Morzine into the southern Swiss canton of Valais, where they speak French. It's often hard to tell which

---

32 The Club eventually replaced its amateur Leaders (like me) with professional instructors (not from the ESF obviously) at some cost.

country you're in when skiing around the PdS - you can often pop in and out of Switzerland several times a day. There are no border controls and, although you're supposed to carry a passport (or suitable ID), no one ever does. If you're off-piste there are no broken black lines in the snow that you'd see on a map denoting the border – there's no way of telling if you're in or outside of the EU.

Cheese is often a useful navigational aid even within France. If you find the tartiflette is made with Abondance cheese, you know you're close to Châtel in the Abondance valley. If it's standard Reblochon, you're probably closer to Avoriaz. If you get Gruyère with your soup, you're probably in Switzerland, if it's Comté, you're probably in France. If you get offered Edam – you're terribly lost. Anyway, back to Zurich Airport.

Due to unforeseen traffic, Vanessa had diverted directly to Laax, leaving me to collect the fourteen members who'd booked the Peak Experience holiday, the name the Club give their holidays for over-fifties. This holiday was called Swiss Bliss, and for members who'd been graded as red/silver on-piste skiers. I later realised a better name would have been 'Pee Experience' given the number of loo stops a bunch of fifty-year-olds need to make on an average day's skiing. It was a sort of singles holiday too, because the package included a single room. The older you get, the less comfortable you are about sharing a room with a stranger. Which, luckily, meant that I too would have a room to myself.

I was looking forward to skiing without having to cook breakfast, wash up and drive down the Cresta Run first. I was also looking forward to skiing somewhere other than the PdS. I was especially looking forward to having a room with a window and ensuite facilities. We would be staying in a four-star hotel, so the bed was unlikely to deflate in the middle of the night, an added bonus.

My first three weeks of Season 6 had been spent battling the Agents of Entropy and *Le Chat Noir*. The Ski Nazis were going to continue the battle and run the chalet for me, while I was away. I was going on an actual skiing holiday (almost) and I was looking forward to the rest.

Earlier that morning I'd caught a train to Zurich from Geneva after a ridiculously early transfer to the station. I'd been up since stupid-o-clock and was shattered.

I love riding on Swiss double-decker trains. There's something childishly exciting about being upstairs on a train. I could say it was because of the better view from the upper deck, but I hauled my skis and heavy bag up the stairs simply to sit there. The journey from Geneva to Zurich crosses almost the entirety of Switzerland in a north-easterly direction and passes some beautiful lakes and breathtaking mountains, but I chose to sleep.

I was woken by a phone call. Vanessa was delayed in traffic and I had to meet the members at the airport on my own and get them onto the transfer coach. I hadn't been expecting to do this and hadn't got a list of their names nor any paperwork. She dictated the list of names to me over a crackly mobile phone connection. She also explained where the transfer bus driver would likely be parked and that he would be looking for her 'Vanessa'. Half asleep, I scribbled some notes on an envelope, which subsequently I could barely read, but I got to Zurich just in time and found the right terminal and the transfer driver. He took some convincing that I was the Vanessa he'd been sent to meet.

I waited with him and my quickly fabricated sign, for the members to arrive. I needed the sign; there were other Leaders waiting to take their charges on different holidays and my blue Leader's jacket would be insufficient to identify me – especially since I was clearly not female.

24. ONE FLEW OVER LAAX

I'm always a little wary when I meet people who are holidaying on their own. I instinctively ask myself, 'Why do they have no friends?' I'm worried that they will try to attach themselves to me and if they succeed, I'll find out why. I've travelled extensively on my own and I'd give myself a wide berth too if I had the misfortune to come across myself. Yet in reality there are many reasons for doing things on your own other than unpopularity. You may have more time and money than your friends or have different interests to your spouse – like skiing for instance. But skiing on your own is dangerous; if you break a leg or get buried under the snow, you're going to want someone to notice. Ski Club holidays are perfect for people without skiing friends (as opposed to no friends at all), or with more spare time and cash than their friends who do ski.

The members started to trickle through from the baggage reclaim. I tried to corral them into a corner of the airport as I ticked them off my almost illegible list. Apart from one lady, who was accompanying her husband, they were all chaps and they all looked a bit dishevelled, having left Gatwick at some ungodly time. They'd probably got out of bed even earlier than me. This could have explained the lack of name recognition when I did the final roll call. I wasn't entirely sure I'd written down all their names correctly and some kept sloping off to the toilet or to find a cash machine and I was uncertain I had everyone until I did a head count on the coach.

They were all ages, shapes and sizes, and had varying amounts of hair. They were all from different socio-economic backgrounds and from different parts of the UK. I led them out of the airport, feeling like Jack Nicholson in *One Flew Over the Cuckoo's Nest*.

They all fell asleep on the coach, some snoring and dribbling, reinforcing my image of Jack's day-out from his asylum. I felt like a tour rep sat in the front seat in my blue jacket next to the driver. Perhaps I should pick up the microphone and give them some information about Laax and the hotel? Except I had none to give. I chose to fall asleep, snoring and dribbling myself.

The driver woke me to ask for directions to the hotel, but I didn't know its name - I really hadn't been expecting to be in charge at this point. I found the hotel's name and address on my phone, and the driver, with my dubious help, located it. It was in Flims, the town next to Laax.

Vanessa, whom I'd never met before, was waiting to greet us. It was a relief to see her blue jacket, not just because it confirmed we were in the right place, but because it meant she could take over being herself.

The hotel could have been an asylum, albeit a very posh Swiss one. It was an imposing white building set in grounds and surrounded by pine trees and what looked like an electric fence. Whether its purpose was to keep the inmates safe from the world or the world safe from the inmates was unclear.

Inside, it had a slight institutional feel and smelt vaguely of cheese. There were alpine touches to the decor, but the vast communal rooms gave it the feel of a conference centre rather than the charming boutique hotel I was expecting. My room was more than comfortable and it had a view of the mountains that forgave its impersonality.

The manager (Jens) made up for the hotel's lack of personality with his own. He was a young, enthusiastic and friendly executive, who was probably working his way up the corporate ladder of the hotel chain. He threw a welcome drinks party that evening where he introduced all his staff and explained the services the hotel had to offer, first in German then in English. It was obvious who was the resident ski instructor: a tanned, tracksuit-wearing Adonis, sporting a mullet.

It's socially hard to meet fourteen people all at one time, to remember their names and where you've got to in the groundhog day conversations you've been having with each other, and I was flagging. I caught up with Vanessa for a pre-dinner briefing. She intended to split the members into two groups and wanted us to head off in the morning, one with each, following our own itinerary, then swap groups each day in turn. This was an alarming proposition that meant I was going to have to lead (not backmark) in a resort I didn't know.

Dinner was a very lengthy and complicated four-course affair. It was a fixed menu with options, all of which had to be ordered in advance. Being old and male, most of the diners, including me, had forgotten what they'd ordered by the time the dishes were served, causing confusion. I, like most blokes, don't put much effort into choosing meals in restaurants, being more interested in the social discourse and I soon forget what I've randomly chosen.

Wine had to be ordered (and paid for) individually, causing yet more confusion. Even more worryingly, none was ordered. The food was 'interesting' and was a fusion of Fawlty Towers' classics such as prawn cocktail, chicken Kiev, and profiteroles, and Bavarian specialties such as bratwursts, sauerkraut, knödel. The cheese board was impressive – we were in Switzerland after all, even if it felt and sounded like Germany most of the time.

I retired early to study the piste map. I'd unwittingly picked up a German version. I couldn't pronounce the names of the lift stations, but the pistes had numbers, not names. '*Das ist good*' I thought. My Denglisch is even worse than my Franglais.

Next morning, breakfast was an international buffet where everything was self-service except the one thing you really needed fast – a caffeine-based hot drink. I didn't want to risk the tea, this being mainland Europe, so I ordered coffee. After more social chitchat, I went to my room and put on my ski gear (my jacket still fitted). Before walking out of the door, I gave the blue doppelganger in the mirror a pep talk: 'remember, as far as *they* know you *are* a good skier.' I then went to the boot room to be greeted by a black cat!

Perhaps the evil cats of this world have some international communication channel and *Le Chat Noir* had been in touch with his Swiss counterpart and asked him to continue his campaign to increase the entropy in my life. This cat belonged to 'Lenny' in as much as any cat can belong to a human – but Lenny fed it.

Lenny was the hotel's shuttle-bus driver and he ferried guests to and from the Flims lift. Although English, he'd lived in Flims for an unspecified number of decades and the cat appeared to be his soulmate. He was a short stocky fellow who would have made a good Bond villain. Others suspected he might be hiding in Switzerland from war crimes, because he was a bit of a fascist about using seatbelts and how skis were secured to his minibus. I introduced myself to him while waiting for the members to show up. He explained the protocols surrounding the service he offered while he stroked the cat.

The first batch of members turned up punctually. To my surprise one of them was carrying telemark skis and the married couple each had a set of blades, the former indicating an off-piste spirit and the latter the intention to stay firmly on-piste. Given the diversity of ability and equipment within the group, it was going to be hard to satisfy all their aspirations. But it was billed as an on-piste holiday and I had my thin, short piste skis so I decided to stick to that.

We all went up the first lift together and, after a couple of runs, Vanessa split the members into two ability groups (fast and slow). She took the fast group, which included the telemarker and I got the slow group, which included the snowblading double act. I headed into the unknown with my charges, following the piste map in my head.

24. ONE FLEW OVER LAAX

When asked what the plan was for the day, I was suitably vague. But, like most well planned resorts, every lift had a blue from the top, so I was unlikely to commit the group to doing an icy black.

In fact, Laax seemed very bereft of scary blacks and the conditions under ski and overhead were superb. The resort wasn't very busy, by French standards at least, and it didn't seem to matter which run I chose because we didn't encounter any bottlenecks or lift queues.

The next day I took the faster group out. I took them on the same route I'd done the previous day, which made me feel like I knew where I was going. I deployed this tactic for most of the week; trying out a route with the slow group then doing it again with the fast group the next day.

The week progressed and my confidence built. The groundhog day conversation evolved and the personalities and banter started to come out, making dinner more socially enjoyable although the confusion over food dragged on.

On the third morning, while at breakfast, Jens announced that it was 'Raclette Night' that evening and we needed to make a reservation if we wanted to pay homage to that famous round cheese. Only Vanessa and I did, so that evening we left the members to continue their culinary adventures in the main dining room and we alone headed towards the smell of Raclette.

I was looking forward to having Vanessa to myself and being able to talk freely with her about Laax, leading, life and cheese, and a few issues that had come up over the last few days – and to having a general bitch about the other inmates.

We followed our noses into the private dining room and discovered it had been turned into a temple for melting cheese. At the altar, behind an enormous Raclette machine was Jens, fully regaled in his lederhosen. The machine was essentially a giant electric fire, akin to a pig roaster – but for cheese. I wondered if the Swiss National Grid needed warning in advance when Jens planned a Raclette Night, so they could bring another generating station online in preparation.

The waitresses were dressed like Heidi and were busy replenishing the vast array of spices, pickles and boiled potatoes that had been assembled on the altar. Wine was ordered and it was soon our turn to receive communion - a scrape of melt from Jens.

Vanessa was charming and an old trooper who had fought many campaigns as a leader. She seemed to have several more leading weeks lined up that season and I began to wonder if I could do the same when I retired from the Chalet Project. Unfortunately, thanks to the ESF, the Club currently had more Leaders than gigs.

We visited the altar several times that evening and every time Jens flicked the machine on, the lights flickered. It was a fun evening that stayed with me for many days afterwards - if you know what I mean.

After a night of weird cheese-related dreams, I woke to find that the weather was closing in. However, that day, I actually had a skiing plan; I intended to summit Laax's highest peak, Vorab (3018m) then ski down its glacier. It would be a shame to leave a resort without getting to its top and my time in Laax was running out.

Despite having the slow group that day, this wasn't as difficult as it sounds, there being a draglift to the top and a red run down the glacier. The route involved ascending the neighbouring peak, Laaxer Stöckli (2898m), and skiing down a wide ridge to the draglift using Piste 28 – a blue run. This wasn't anything like the Vallée Blanche in Chamonix, where glacier skiing needs a proper guide.

We boarded the bubble that ascends Laaxer Stöckli and the visibility was good, despite some high-level cloud cover. But when we got off at the top it was appalling - we stepped into a cloud.

Unlike fog that hangs in a valley on a still day, the inside of a cloud is white and turbulent. It is full of water vapour that crystallises on your goggles and other flat surfaces. Anything that moves becomes a centre of crystallisation. You're effectively making your own snow while you move through a cloud and you have to keep scraping the crystals off your goggles in order to see. You sometimes don't realise just how *local* the poor visibility is and it's often confined to the inside of your goggles. To make things worse, when you stop the inside of your goggles mists up with condensation. Once you start moving, if the goggles are well designed, air starts circulating inside them and they become less opaque. Often it's a good idea to just launch yourself down a slope blind, hoping your goggles will clear before you hit something.

There was little point in continuing on our journey to the glacier. The reason for wanting to go up Vorab was to see the views not just to summit Laax. The sensible thing would have been to jump back on the bubble and head down and ski some lower slopes. However, riding lifts *down* was an anathema to the Ski Nazi and I had been well indoctrinated. I would feel a great deal of shame, if they ever found out, and I'd possibly lose respect from any latent Ski Nazis in my group.

While I deliberated whether I could find the start of the blue, and if the poor visibility was just localized, other skiers got off the bubble and headed off into the cloud, presumably they were locals and knew its location, so I decided to follow them.

They led me to the first piste marker of Run 28 and I could see a further two ahead reassuring me that it would be possible to follow the piste back down to Vorab's lower station. The group had started to string out behind me so I kept stopping, losing my impromptu pathfinders. The piste then took a small zigzag, not big enough to be marked on the map – and I went straight on, faithfully followed by the rest.

I soon realised my mistake, because the snow under-ski became unpisted and I couldn't see the next marker pole. Normally, when you can't see the next marker pole, you can follow the curb left by the basher[33] that made the piste – but there wasn't one. It either didn't exist, because the basher hadn't been down the run recently, or I'd crossed it without noticing some way back.

The gang bunched up behind me and I debated with the Ski Demons on which was the least risky direction to go. I knew that we were on a ridge, albeit a wide one, and some serious drops where not too far away on either side. The sensible thing might be to retrace our steps, but deciding to go uphill is never very popular. Then I got a brief glimpse of what might have been a skier so I decided to head in their direction.

This wasn't exactly an ideal situation. I had no knowledge of the run, so couldn't navigate via memory, I was off-piste with cliffs either side, there were no piste markers in sight, and I was relying on an apparition in the mist on the assumption that it wasn't lost too.

Mercifully I spotted a piste marker, skied over to it and gave it a big hug. Then I wacked it with my ski pole to shake off the ice crystals revealing a large orange band. Now another dilemma presented itself: I couldn't remember with any certainty if that meant it was a left or right marker pole. We were definitely still in Switzerland, we hadn't gone that badly wrong, but I'd forgotten which way round the Swiss marked their poles and there was no discernible curb to indicate which side of the pole had been pisted. I made a guess based on the wind direction, assuming it was a westerly and I knew the piste headed generally in an easterly direction - then the cavalry arrived.

A piste patroller skied up to the pole and gave it another whack. I was very pleased to see him and we exchanged pleasantries in

---

33 A Piste **Basher** is a Caterpillar driven snowplough that flattens the pistes, usually at night. The Austrians used to run them in the day too, but this caused too many deaths. I've had a few scares myself, when skiing round a bend to find the shovel of a plough blocking my way.

Denglisch and he pointed at my goggles and gesticulated that I needed to clear them. The visibility immediately improved. He headed off and I seized the opportunity to follow him. Luckily he kept stopping to whack each marker pole as he passed. Then my next dilemma occurred.

Unfortunately, the gang had strung out again and I lost sight of a couple at the back. I stopped and waited for them, while reluctantly watching another impromptu guide disappear into the distance. I started to worry about the length of time the tail-ender was taking to materialise. After ten minutes, I was getting very worried. Had he skied past me, or skied off a cliff, or had he fallen and been injured? How long should I wait before acting? Everyone was getting cold.

He finally turned up; he'd been helping someone else recover from a fall. I headed in the general direction I'd seen the patroller go and celebrated each time the next pole came into sight. Finally, out of the mist, a lift station revealed itself. I was very relieved to see it – even though I wasn't sure which one it was. Once identified, I could determine my location on the map and come up with a plan to find the fastest way out of the cloud. I decided to go down in the cable car – to hell with the shame.

Next day, the weather was perfect and, it being the last day of the holiday, the two groups met for lunch. A posh restaurant in Larnags, a hamlet some distance from Flims, had been booked. It was nice to end the week with a long lunch in a nice restaurant but everyone paid individually, meaning it was quite some time before we remounted our skis.

No time was left for anything other than to ski directly home. Vanessa took those who wanted a last blast down an off-piste route. This left me to lead the rest home, down the run to Flims (Piste 66). Shortly after we parted company, I noticed her stop and start waving at me. I put this down to friendliness - then I got a text from her. I stopped and read it. 'Last bubble Plaun 4:15!!'

Then I realised what all the waving had been about. I'd inadvertently taken a right fork and was heading back to Larnags and was likely to be catching a taxi home from there - well two taxis because there were eight of us, which would be expensive and, more importantly, embarrassing. It meant I had blown it on the last day of my first week of Ski Club leading. The ability to reliably get members home on skis, was a minimum prerequisite for any Leader.

So I cracked the whip on my already tired group and we sprinted back to Larnags, barged to the front of the lift queue and made it back to the top of Route 66 with fifteen minutes to go before the Plaun Bubble closed. This wasn't long enough for the tail-enders to descend the mogul covered red, so I abandoned my charges and bolted for the lift. I got there as it was closing and pleaded with the lifties (or whatever they're called in German – die lifties?) Initially they thought I was in need of medical attention, I was puffing and panting and babbling on in Denglisch. Luckily, Swiss *die lifties* are far more accommodating than their French counterparts, whom I was more accustomed to, and they waited for everyone to filter down. We jumped into the penultimate bubble to descend that afternoon and *die lifties* into the last.

That evening, after the final dinner, Vanessa and I were presented with a thank-you card and a large tip, which was very gratifying, and unusually thoughtful for a bunch of blokes. I spent mine buying brandy for the guys and myself, finally letting my metaphorical hair down. One or two of them even bought a copy of my book.

In the morning, there was one last piece of official business to take care of – reviewing the members' ski grades. For the first time in my life I was to be a judge rather than be judged. I bowed to Vanessa's superior experience and interpretation of the Club's grading system in most cases. Being a wise old owl, she left it to me to hand out the grading cards on the transfer bus back to the airport; she was heading to her next Ski Club gig by car.

24. ONE FLEW OVER LAAX

I wasn't looking forward to the bus ride. It would involve long and subjective discussions about each individual's skiing ability, based on the Club's somewhat esoteric definition of what a 'good skier' actually meant. I decided that cowardice was the best option, and waited until we arrived before swiftly handing out the cards. Then I said my goodbyes and legged it for the train station. The misdiagnosed lunatics were headed back to their asylums and I was heading back to mine – Chalet Framboise.

There was plenty of time for reflection as the train wound its way back to Geneva but the Swiss banker sitting opposite me interrupted my thoughts. He was having a loud and lengthy phone conversation with his divorce lawyer (in English). By the end of the journey I was rooting for his wife, although it sounded like she'd married well.

From an existential perspective, freedom cannot be separated from responsibility, even though people seek freedom while trying to avoid responsibility and I am certainly guilty of that. While leading in Laax, I had been free to press on to the top of Vorab. Despite the conditions, I had still wanted to achieve my goal; and my group had conceded their freedom by following me up, making me responsible for them. Even if you ski alone, you put others in jeopardy - those forced to mount a rescue, should you not return. When you're free to make choices, you take on responsibility not only for yourself. The consequences of our choices are not always so obvious – especially on those we love.

On a lighter note, I concluded that my first week as a Leader had gone reasonably well. Nobody had been lost or injured and nobody had skied off a cliff. Most importantly, nobody had needed to catch a taxi home. I'd also made a lot of new friends and become a fan of Raclette, Laax and lederhosen.

Over the next few weeks the feedback from the guys rolled in via the Club's website and not all of it was bad. Although the runner I did at the airport had obviously brought some of their marks down. And the Club asked me to lead in Laax the following year, so I must have done okay. Next time they wanted me to be the head Leader – I was going to play Vanessa for real.

25. Women Behaving Badly

It was 3am and for the fifth night in a row, I'd sat up into the small hours waiting for my phone to ring. I'd watched just about every palatable film on Netflix and had started to reassess the ones I'd rejected earlier in the week. I couldn't go to bed because there wasn't a signal in the laundry and even if there had been, I couldn't be sure my phone would wake me up.

I was waiting for the evacuation call - a plea to extract survivors from the streets of Morzine. I only hoped that I could get enough sense out of one of them to tell me exactly which street they needed scooping up from. I consoled myself with the thought that I wasn't in the Buddha Bar myself. I also knew I wouldn't have to serve breakfast particularly early, unless you count making bacon sandwiches at 4am as breakfast.

'Scouse Week' was almost over and frankly I was getting too old to host my favourite ladies from Liverpool. Shiv and her female mates had been supporters of the Project since its inception and their annual visit had always provided the highlight (and lowlight) of my alcoholic season.

It had been the first Scouse Week in Chalet Framboise and probably the last, which was an equally sad and happy thought. The chalet clearly didn't suit their *modus operandi*. It would take forty minutes to walk home to Chalet Framboise in a straight line from the bars of Morzine and infinitely longer if drunk. It was uphill too, so gravity would hinder not help them. Gravity seems to get stronger when you're drunk. I always end up at the bottom of things: a bar, a basement, a basket, a bottle or a bunk.

My study of cougars in their natural habitat had been fascinating. I'd lived amongst them and been accepted into their pride. But that aspect of the Project was drawing to its natural end. It was time to write the article and submit it to *National Geographic*. I had to be careful to protect the guilty and not reveal their identities nor break the chalet host's golden rule - 'what goes on tour …'

Shiv's mates were not all cougars technically; some were happily married with kids, if such a state can exist, others were divorced and one was actually a bloke. After five seasons, they were all my mates now too, and I knew they felt bad about keeping me up and would probably stay elsewhere next season.

They really came to Morzine to surf not to ski. They did ski during their downtime, when the sun was up, but their main sport, surfing blokes, was nocturnal. They came to surf the myriad of men in Morzine for their annual drinking trip to the Alps. January was best time of year for this activity, the surf was always 'up' and Morzine became Manzine.

Those pretending to be cougars were always the most relentless. When a busy mum is let off her leash she has no time for sleeping. Her alter ego needs to live its life in one short week and enjoy all the male attention – even if quite a lot of it is unwanted.

It's often hard for a lady (cougar or not) to break off the encounter from an unwanted suitor without being rude. Shiv often uses the Buddhist *mudra* for prayer (hands pressed together held close to the chest). One drunken Australian noticed and asked, 'what the hell does that mean?' pointing to her hands. 'Oh, in Liverpool this means fuck off' she answered. He laughed and continued regardless – in true tenacious Ozzie style.

I no longer went drinking with my friends. It had taken five seasons, but I no longer wanted to party with two hundred drunk men and thirty drunk women in a noisy bar. It wasn't the odds that I minded so much, but I was done with meeting and competing for airspace with the other drunken raconteurs. In any case, since meeting Debbie I was truly out of the game.

Thanks to the location of Framboise, I always had to drive. Many Saga Louts drink a 'safe' amount and drive but I was no longer prepared to do even that. Not just because it was irresponsible and illegal, although they were reasons enough, but because the drive up to Framboise was dangerous and the Cresta Run was challenging enough when completely sober. To enjoy such evenings I would have to raise my alcohol level well past the legal limit, passing my existential limit on the way. Even if I didn't get breathalysed and arrested, I would wake up in another type of prison cell.

I was also going deaf – which made drinking as an observer sport less fun. Not being able to hear the conversations above the shouting Saga Louts was frustrating even if I'd heard most of them before.

The previous season, while doing some final research, I noticed a cougar (from a different pride) playing the *femme fatale* expertly. She was alternately chatting up two different groups of Saga Louts at alternate ends of the bar. While thinking it must be hard to keep track of two flirtatious conversations simultaneously, I noticed she was having a third with her pride. Shortly after accepting drinks from one prey herd, the pride left with the other, leaving disappointed faces and amusement on mine. It was all very light-hearted – the blokes knew the game. However, I've never seen a cougar working a bar with such precision.

During my research, I've been introduced to dozens of men by Shiv. It's always impressive how she remembers all their names. Usually, they didn't really want to talk to me and I didn't really want to drink with them. I get enough groundhog day conversation making small talk with new guests.

Often the initial conversation would be an inquest into why the girls had failed to turn up for skiing or lunch that day - why, as the French say, they had sent a rabbit instead (*poser un lapin*).

During that final Scouse Week, I still managed to do some Girlfriend Skiing with the cougars and eat several epic alfresco lunches. It's good to 'be done by noon and drunk by three,' as Hemingway once pointed out.

GF skiing can sometimes get exciting if lunch goes past 3pm. We often find ourselves racing for connecting lifts, if we don't want to catch a taxi back to Morzine. It's amazing how fast the girls can ski once they get a bottle of rosé on-board.

Sometimes they make unilateral arrangements for skiing and lunch the previous evening – arrangements they actually want to keep. To save someone getting disappointed they often try to amalgamate their daytime plans.

Naturally people want to ski and have lunch with their friends – new and old - but the ideal number for a skiing date is two. However, when flocks merge into murmurations they become impossible to steer. Most starlings have a similar flying ability, but within a skiing murmuration there will always be a mixture of abilities and they never last long. It's also difficult to book a lunch table big enough for everyone - even if you do manage it, half of the flocks won't turn up.

I noticed during my study, that murmurations also often occur at après time. They can be seen most often in March, when cougars are at their most active and the drinking can be done outside. I'd often find myself in a 'super group' of blokes after skiing. Shiv would introduce everyone and sometimes they would all hit it off, although sometimes not.

I'm always impressed that the girls can remember so many names. One week Shiv alone introduced me to seven 'Daves'. I thought she might be specialising in Davids to simplify her life.

After one particularly well attended après session, I asked the girls how they remembered so many names and which Dave they were currently talking about on the way home. They seem to use the most noticeable attribute of the individual or at least the most important to them. There was tall Dave, short Dave, bald Dave, gropy Dave, banker Dave, halitosis Dave and fit Dave – interestingly I immediately knew which Dave they meant.

Often during après the group would splinter, making it hard for the pride to reassemble. They would have different degrees of reluctance to leave depending on how much fun they were having. However, they all had to get back to the chalet eventually, in order to prepare for the next phase of the evening – eating (optional), getting showered (optional) and going out again (mandatory). Once home, some snacked and some rested. Usually it was around 10pm before they were all ready to go back into action – and once more unto the breach.

One of the main attractions of a skiing holiday is that there's no pressure to dress up when going out. Unlike going out in Liverpool, there's no need to dress to kill. Jeans, a clean T-shirt and trainers are all that's really required – anything else and you'll look over-dressed. Even when I'm going to a posh restaurant I don't feel the need to wear heels or a skirt.

The stated reason for going out so late was that the Buddha Bar didn't really get going till midnight – presumably because until then the blokes would be too sober and shy. Monitoring the ebb and flow of Morzine's nightlife, which bar to be in and when, is another study of its own.

During Scouse Week there's usually little enthusiasm for eating out in the evening – especially after a big lunch. Along with the unnecessary calories, it's generally regarded as a waste of money and time, and can involve being potentially stuck with a small and possibly the wrong group of chaps. Occasionally, after consulting with me, they would invite blokes round to the chalet for dinner. I didn't mind, assuming halitosis Dave wasn't invited - in fact I encouraged it. It wasn't only more profitable, if I remembered to charge, but if I supplied enough wine they wouldn't want to go out at ten; I could drink too and go to bed when I liked.

It's possible to find true love in the Buddha. One barmaid fell in love with a punter and moved back to the UK. Another couple I know met there and made a life in Morzine. And let's not forget I met Dr Debs skiing. Although, our eyes didn't exactly meet for the first time in the Buddha Bar, we certainly visited the place. I don't want to do the Buddha a disservice; I actually really like the bar. You've just got to be there at the right time and in the right mental state – drunk.

You might think my cougar study has too small a data set to be scientifically valid but my observations are also based on another pride of cougars - Morzine Mary and the MILFs.[34] Slightly older and wiser now, they've behaved worse in their time. They were

---

34 In this context, **MILF** stands for Morzine International Ladies Federation; although the majority of them were from the same sovereign state (Liverpool) and most members are mothers, if not grandmothers by now.

probably the first female pioneers of Manzine; they've seen and done it all before.

They once decided to put Post-It notes on the backs of their prey. They gave all the blokes in the bar a score out of ten for handsomeness, then wrote the score on a note and covertly attached it. Soon, nearly every man in the bar was wearing a number. One chap noticed and accused the MILFs of being the perpetrators. 'What makes you think it was us, Mr 2?', was the reply.

In the MILFs defence they were very generous and seldom handed out a score less than six – which I thought was, in some cases, very kind. Now, whenever I get a glimpse of yellow in a woman's handbag, I check my back in the mirror every time I go to the gents.

I've also added many individual observations to my data set. For instance, I once overheard a non-affiliated cougar say, 'If you can remember my name, I'll snog you'. After seeing her suitor's frustrated look, she added, 'I'll give you a clue, it's Fay.' Another, having accidentally been elbowed by a passing waiter, shouted, 'If your dick's as hard as your elbow, I'm staying at the Rhodos - room 103'.

But, Scouse Week is no more and my article has been filed. I'll miss the company of my favourite Liverpudlians and their laughter, if not their hi-pitched shrieks and the headache induced by listening to estuary squawk for seven consecutive days. I'll miss their alfresco lunches and Girlfriend Skiing *en masse*.

Chalet Framboise may not have worked for them, but it certainly worked for me. I'm just that bit older than they are and maybe they'll soon catch up and be happy to return to me, having changed their annual week of hedonism for an actual skiing holiday.

When a bloke hangs out with ladies on tour, he often finds out things it might have been best for him not to know. His opinions on beards, bums, bellies, biceps, bulging wallets and behaviour will all be challenged. I now know what makes men attractive to women and what turns them off – mostly everything we wear, do or say.

My opinions are undoubtedly sexist, but sexism works both ways. In Manzine the usual roles are uniquely reversed but the men are willing victims and seldom complain. What's the point of a girls' trip, or indeed a boys' one, if you can't drink too much, behave badly, and flirt with the opposite sex?

26. A Bad Bout of Entropy

If you're a true fan, you'll remember where and what you were doing when you heard that David Bowie had died. I was sitting on the chalet sofa watching Sky News. It didn't help that I was in the paranoia phase of a category eight hangover, but Life on Mars (and Earth) had to go on. Fortunately, someone else was cooking breakfast for the guests that morning.

A guest (Nigel) had volunteered to cook breakfast for everyone the previous evening. He'd voiced an interest in being one of my substitute chalet hosts – I needed cover when I went on Ski Club leading duties. I'd cunningly suggested he did some work experience that morning.

Fortunately, he had taken the Hemingway Oath[35] and got up early and started cooking. He passed the 'cooking a fry with a hangover' test with flying colours - but that was the only break the Agents of Entropy would give me that day.

While he was clearing up, I went outside to liberate Landie from the overnight snowfall and found *Le Chat Noir* on her bonnet and, needless to say, Landie wouldn't start. Perhaps it wasn't the cat's fault, unless it had deliberately given Landie the sad news. For five years, Landie and I had driven up and down France listening to Bowie's music. I should have anticipated the anthropomorphic grief and granted her a compassionate day off.

I went through my usual routine of replacing the fuel filter and priming the fuel pump, suspecting they were frozen, but nothing would work. So I summoned the local breakdown garage, via the AA international call centre, a procedure I was familiar with.

---

[35] Hemingway once said, 'Always do sober what you said you'd do drunk. That will teach you to keep your mouth shut.' Once you agree to abide by this rule, you have taken the **Hemingway Oath.**

The guests walked down the Cresta Run to the bus stop carrying their skis and left me and the cat to get on with it.

We spent most of the morning watching the French 'AA man' try to work out what was wrong with the English relic. Then, presumably fed up of speaking Franglais with me while being stared at by an evil cat, he decided to take Landie to his garage.

He (we) had a hell of a job getting the patient onto the back of his flatbed truck, which was only slightly bigger than Landie. He was parked on the Cresta Run and Landie was on firmer ground. Whenever he turned the winch on, his truck was dragged towards Landie rather than the other way round.

With Landie finally loaded and dispatched, I called the AA to arrange a replacement hire car. After much negotiation, I convinced the call centre that a Peugeot 208 with summer tyres wasn't going to suit my needs and a suitable replacement vehicle was finally found in Evian (forty kilometres away). But I had to go and collect it.

It's a little-known fact (or so it seems) that the water in the River *Dranse*, which runs through Morzine, enters Lake Geneva at *Évian-Les-Bains*. They put it in plastic bottles there and send them round the world for people with too much money to drink. I always smile when guests enter the chalet with bottles of the stuff. I point at the kitchen sink and inform them that I have *Évian* on tap.

A taxi was summoned from Évian to take me to the car-rental office. The driver's English was non-existent and giving him directions over the phone was *très difficile* in Franglais.

He eventually found me and sensibly didn't attempt an uphill accent of the Cresta Run, but collected me at the bottom.

We made it to the hire car garage just as they closed for lunch. I wandered around *Évian* for two hours, drinking their fine water in an attempt to rehydrate. By this time my hangover had moved from the paranoia phase into the existential self-loathing phase and I reflected on life, Land Rovers, the universe and everything else.

When the garage reopened, I went in and introduced myself. The nice lady didn't speak English either but I thought she was implying that I had to leave a deposit of 'un mille euros'! I asked her to write the number down, because I thought the word 'mille' meant 1,000.

To my horror she wrote a one and then three zeros on a scrap of paper. I told her I wanted to hire a car not buy one, but my humour was lost in translation. I wasn't sure my French credit card would stand that amount. It didn't, so I used a combination of cards and cash.

As is customary in France the paperwork took longer than the job it pertained to and it wasn't until 4pm that I was ready to depart. I should have meticulously examined the car for existing dents but it was quickly being covered in fresh snow along with the roads and I was in a rush to get back to Morzine while I still could.

I got back just in time to pick up some of my guests from an après bar and tell them dinner in the chalet was off. I'd been sourcing a replacement vehicle all day and hadn't had time to cook – fortunately they were very understanding. I took them to a restaurant and I headed back to the chalet to regroup. I forgot I wasn't in Landie and headed directly up the Cresta Run at full speed – then promptly slid off the side embedding my precious hire-car in a pile of snow left by the plough.

Livid for making myself vehicle-less for a second time in one day, I walked up to the chalet and asked those who had made it home on their own, expecting to eat dinner, to come and push me out instead.

At this stage, my brain had stopped working; I'd gone into full panic mode. We tried to push the car up the hill rather than back down. I was concerned that the rear right wheel would slide further off the edge and ground the back axle – and I would lose my €1,000 deposit.

It was now dark and the snow had turned into a blizzard making communication above the wind difficult. We decided to put the car's snow chains on, but being unfamiliar with them, we could only get one fitted. I used my iPhone as a torch and must have put it down on the snow while struggling to put the second chain on.

The real problem was that I was in charge and by that point I wasn't thinking clearly. It would have been better if someone else had taken command. After another ten minutes of struggling with the chains, everyone's fingers had become numb and I decided I'd better call the guests in town and tell them to get a taxi home – often a difficult task. But I couldn't find my phone. It had either been covered by fresh snowfall or buried during the frantic digging we'd done around the car.

Once I'd realise that my phone (and my life) was lost, all resources - people, time and remaining cognitive powers - were diverted from liberating the car to finding the phone. We did the usual things: retraced my steps, rang the phone, used 'find-my-iPhone'; none of them worked. We could barely hear each other, let alone hear a phone ringing outside and the Apple website seemed to think it was 100m away down a gorge.

I recalled using the phone in the car just prior to getting stuck. It couldn't be there unless I'd thrown it out of the window and, even in my current metal state, I *would* have remembered doing that.

The usual pointless question was asked: 'Where did you last have it?' prompting the usual sarcastic answer, 'If I knew that, it wouldn't be bloody lost would it?' Once you lose your sense of humour, all is lost - and I had.

So I decided to abandon the search along with the car and invoke my 'lost phone backup plan'. I had a spare phone and even a spare SIM card – it would be operational with my existing number by the morning.

Having given up on life and on extracting the car, even though it was partially blocking the road, I downed a couple of glasses of red (maybe a bottle) and collapsed onto my airbed in the laundry - but I landed with a familiar thump. *Le Chat Noir* had been in and punctured it. I had no plan C for this and I accepted my uncomfortable fate.

If ever I wanted to take up smoking again, now was it. So I reached for my vaping pipe, which I keep for moments of weakness - and dropped it onto the tile floor where it shattered rendering it inoperable. I forced myself to laugh and planned a fitting revenge on the bloody cat.

I woke up at 7am the next morning rather stiff. Initially I thought I'd had a really bad dream until I saw my old phone next to me and noticed that my mattress was flat.

At least the old phone was working; I'd had a text message from Debbie wondering why there had been a telecommunications blackout the night before. Then I remembered the predicament I'd left the hire car in and that it was probably blocking the road. I was worried the snowplough might turn up and push it off the side or that it would prevent my neighbours from getting to work.

I leapt up and got dressed, in a hurry to find out. Still pulling clothes on, I walked through the living room to see that the Agents of Entropy had not stopped their campaign just because I'd gone to bed. The ceiling was covered in red wine marks - I must have missed a hell of a party, I thought. Then I stepped in some cat sick walking through the kitchen.

I went outside and waded to the car in a foot of fresh snow. With a clearer head and in daylight I thought I could get the second chain on and reverse down the road, just risking the back axle grounding – it seemed so obvious suddenly.

Before I'd started on the second chain, a white Land Rover Defender with French number plates appeared on the road above me. Maybe God did exist and he had sent me a brother, a fellow Landie owner, to pull me out. I'd used mine to pull countless mortals out of tricky situations; the good karma must finally have come around.

The driver rolled down his window to reveal he was wearing an ESF jacket. I approached expecting some international Land Rover kinship, forgetting I was stood in front of a Toyota, but no offer of assistance was forthcoming, just a torrent of abuse in French.

I'm not exactly sure what he said. I recognised a few French swear words and worked out that the gist of his sentiment was mostly about my parentage. I tried to apologise in Franglais, thus revealing my true identity - an English fuck-wit.

Impressively he repeated his entire rant in English. *'I am zee head of the ESF in Avoriaz, I'm late for an important meeting with over a hundred instructors. If you don't get sis car out of my way, I'll shunt it down zee hill!'* He informed me.

He started revving his engine, but I knew this was an idle threat because his pristine Defender was highly polished and not the sort you'd use as a ram - unlike mine. I tried to explain I hadn't parked, but got stuck. If he gave me a few minutes, I'd get my other chain on and be out of his way – I was entirely certain this was true.

Unfortunately, I found putting on a snow chain while being chastised by an irate Frenchman, was even more difficult than doing it in the dark - so I gave up. I jumped in, slammed the car into reverse and floored the throttle. I couldn't see out of the rear windows, I'd not been given time to clear that or the rear side window.

To my delight the car popped out of its snowy tomb and we started to career down the Cresta Run backwards completely blind. I wound down the driver's window and could see the edge of the road so used that for a trajectory guide. All I could see through the small clearing I'd made on the windscreen was a looming white Defender with an apoplectic Gallic face still ranting obscenities inside.

Before the impromptu car-train reached the bottom, he violently turned off the road and over took me off-piste. He hit the main road and was gone. I was very impressed with his driving and wondered what tyres he was using and where I could get some for Landie.

My exit from the Cresta Run, although done backwards, was less spectacular. I might have scored more points than him for doing it effectively blindfolded, but he did it with typically French style.

The phone rang. Landie must be fixed and I thought, finally, the worst bout of entropy I've ever had in my life was over. All I had to do was drive back to Evian, clean and return the hire car full of fuel (as instructed), then cab it over to the AA garage. Miraculously, it looked like I wouldn't lose my deposit because the hire car still looked intact.

While cleaning the car at a jet wash, I notice a large dent in the bonnet. Unless a very small boulder had come down in the night, this was some pre-hire damage that I'd not spotted. While driving over to the hire company I prepared myself for a Franglais argument. I rehearsed the line, '*il n'a pas* été *moi*' – it wasn't me. When I handed the keys back the nice lady inspected the car while I tried to look nonchalant preparing to mimic surprise. Mercifully, she didn't notice the dent.

I picked up Landie, to find that all that was wrong was a loose wire – but it had still cost 150 euros to repair. I tried to find out for future reference, which wire it was that had come loose, but my French wasn't good enough to ask and it's still a mystery to me to this day. Perhaps I should ask the cat?

On the way back, my old phone rang again. It was Debbie and it was calming to hear her familiar voice. 'So how was your day darling?' she asked.

I told her about the events of the last twenty four hours which must have come over as a rant. I concluded that I was losing my mind and I hadn't brought a backup brain to France. I also needed a ball of string to tie important things to me - and a gun for killing cats.

I spent the afternoon listening to David Bowie while cooking an arrival meal for my next set of guests, which had a calming effect. I cleaned the cat sick up and the red wine off the ceiling then ordered another airbed online – my life was back on track. I concluded that I must always keep a sense of humour no matter what happens in order to mentally survive. No matter how dark your day gets, the sun will eventually rise.

Three months later, I found myself walking down the Cresta Run at 2am in the morning. The stars were out in force and, not being able to sleep, I'd decided to take the rubbish down to the communal bins at the bottom. It was a warm evening and I walked down in my slippers and dressing gown, looking like a ghostly apparition, gazing up at the stars.

The breath-taking views in the Alps don't always stop when the sun goes down. The stars are that bit closer and with little air or light pollution, at night they can be seen in all their celestial glory. If you're lucky, and the sky is clear on the night of a super moon,[36] the mountains become floodlit and then it becomes very tempting to lay down in the snow and just stare up in wonder – especially after a few drinks.

On that night, while briefly looking down, I noticed the top of my lost phone sticking out of a melting block of ice on the verge.

---

36 A **supermoon** or perigee-syzygy as it's technically known occurs when the Moon, thanks to the gravitational effects of other celestial bodies, is closer than normal to the Earth.

It looked like a mini glacier offering up its dead. It was more or less where my hire-car wheel had got stuck. So, after all, I'd not suffered temporary insanity as Apple had suggested, and thrown it down a gorge. Although the screen was shattered, amazingly, after charging, it still worked!

27. The French Door Test

I was busy in the kitchen 'repairing' dinner - I was re-thatching my tartiflette with new cheese, replacing the original thatch that had burnt. While doing so, I heard Sarah shriek, 'A strange man has just run upstairs!'

Everyone laughed at her but Sarah was relatively sober and a relatively sensible person so I had to take her seriously. The front door at Chalet Neige was usually left open; its handle was too difficult for most guests to operate and I'd got tired of explaining how it worked.

If the front door was locked and nobody was in, the opening procedure involved retrieving the key from the key safe, which meant remembering its location and the code to open it, which required a torch at night. This was way too complicated for most drunks, so I used to have a policy of always leaving the front door unlocked. Even then, some battled for hours trying to unlock the unlocked door until I got up and opened it for them. To be fair, the door was a bit stiff and gave a good impression of being locked when it wasn't. Even when the operative was sober, the handle needed raising to the vertical for the key to rotate, so locking the door also seemed beyond the wit of most people.

The intruder must be John, I thought. He'd checked in while Sarah was out and they hadn't been introduced, but I did think it strange that he hadn't said hello. I grabbed the poker from the fire and nervously climbed the stairs to the bedroom floor. One door was shut and I could hear rustling in the room behind it.

27. THE FRENCH DOOR TEST

I summoned the other guests and they lined up behind me, brandishing a selection of weapons – most had grabbed kitchen utensils and even in the right hands most of them would not have been especially lethal. We burst into the room to find John lying on the bed wearing only his boxer shorts and a startled face. Everyone dropped their weapons and I did the introductions – which was rather awkward for everyone concerned.

I asked why he'd snuck in and not said hello. He slurred something about Robo's and Old Lager, the insanely strong beer from Mützig, and all became clear - he was too drunk for human interaction and had taken himself to bed.

'Where's Phil?' I asked. The two forty-somethings had arrived earlier then left together to meet some cronies in the notorious Bar Robinson. Apparently John had left Phil there to complete the Mützig challenge – seven pints in one night. Which was tough considering it opens at 5pm and closes again at 8pm.

Reportedly Phil, a rugby-playing Cornishman, finished an impressive eighth pint of the loopy-juice, stood up, shouted, 'I laugh in the face of Mützig,' then left the bar and promptly fell over in the snow outside. He then crawled to the bench, which had been considerately positioned by the proprietor next to the door, and waited for the feeling in his legs to come back. Phil eventually made it back to the chalet and went straight upstairs too, although he at least managed a 'hello' – or at least that's what I think he said.

Later that season, during Scouse Week, I had a genuine intruder. A group of Welsh lads had rented the chalet opposite. After seeing the girls having dinner through the window, one lad decided to stagger into our chalet to join them. I looked up from my end of the table to see him chatting to one of the girls at the other end. It took a few moments for us to realise that nobody knew him and nobody had invited him in. He was too young for even a cougar and no one knew his name – he wasn't able to recall it himself.

I gently escorted him to the door and locked it. We spent the night under siege because he returned with his pals, pleading to be let in. I agreed to drive them into town, knowing they wouldn't find their way back. Unfortunately, some did and knocked on the door again in the small hours, this time driven by desperation not lust - they couldn't open their own front door. I showed them how and went to bed irritated. I'd got enough on my hands looking after my own drunks without having to look after those belonging to the neighbours.

My open-door policy used to worry many guests – mostly those who lived in cities. I didn't worry much about security in Morzine, although I know the number of burglaries has risen since the time when the locals used to keep their valuables in sheds. I also know, that once you've been burgled, you become paranoid. However, I still don't know why people bring expensive items: watches, jewellery, hats, coats and gloves; they're just a liability when skiing and drinking. In fact, generally I don't know why people buy things that cost more than can be justified by their quality. I can't lose or smash my Rolex – because I haven't got one. Generally, possessions make us a prison; they end up owning us, because we have to spend so much time trying to protect and keep them safe. Anyway, that's enough Marxist theory.

In my experience British people commonly have problems opening doors in France. Many years ago, when I still went on Lads' Trips, I found myself leaving Dick's Tea Bar, a nightclub in *Méribel*, on my own. Being older than the others and married, I'd had enough and left them to it. Despite some navigational issues, I found the right chalet and managed to open the door with the key that had been entrusted to me. I'd actually insisted on

27. THE FRENCH DOOR TEST

being the key holder, to prevent being held hostage in a club by Andy because he'd pulled that stunt on me before. As promised, I dutifully left the door unlocked.

Matt was the next to bail - he'd obviously had enough 'tea' too. On his return, slightly debilitated by alcohol, he couldn't work out how to open the door and assumed it was locked although it was just a bit stiff. He'd gone out appropriately dressed for a nightclub, but not for standing in a blizzard shouting at a window trying to wake his unconscious friend. In desperation he threw a fire extinguisher, of unknown origin, through a window and climbed in.

This *did* wake me up and I leapt out of bed and ran downstairs to see Matt drawing the curtains behind him in the hope I wouldn't notice that the glass was missing. I certainly did because the chalet turned into an icebox. Andy, on his return, equally debilitated, decided we needed a fire and wasn't going to let the absence of logs stop him. Being a Neanderthal, he smashed up a coffee table and set it alight in the wood burner.

The next day, Matt reported the broken window to the letting agent who then noticed that the coffee table was missing and called the gendarmes! It looked like we weren't going skiing that day.

The police arrived and we all sat round the remaining dining table. I listened in disbelief while Matt explained to the officer, who spoke English, how the window had been broken by a gang of delinquent French youths who'd followed him home. They'd thrown the fire extinguisher through the window and stolen the table!

When the policeman asked me to corroborate Matt's story, I explained I was upstairs asleep and saw nothing. The awkward silence that followed gave me time to compare the earnest expression on Matt's face with the look of incredulity on the officer's. In between I caught a distant glimpse of a charred table leg still smouldering in the wood burner - I vowed I'd never go on a lads' ski trip ever again.

Those paranoid about crime often lock up their skis every time they leave them. Some like to mispair their skis with a friend's when leaving them outside a mountain restaurant in order to confuse villains. Although I must admit, it's common for people to mistakenly take the wrong skis from a rack if they've just hired them. There have been a couple of occasions when I've looked down and noticed guests trying to mount the wrong pair of skis. Once I got home to find a pair of skis from the wrong hire shop on my roof rack. Although a simple mistake, it can leave the rightful owner stranded on the mountain and is regarded as a very serious crime, especially by the Swiss police. A friend and I almost got arrested when he made a similar mistake in Zermatt – unfortunately for us the skis belonged to the mayor!

I know now that Matt was an Agent of Entropy along with Andy his accomplice in *Méribel*. His failure to operate a French front door was the clue. After the Welsh incident, I started locking the chalet doors at night and I began to notice that the people who were unable to lock and unlock the front door usually turned out to be Agents of Entropy.

I noticed that Agents also seemed to have great problems operating the French windows onto the chalet's balcony. I know, in France all windows are French, but the ones commonly found in France have even more complicated functionality than French door handles. Every time I tried to explain to an outwardly intelligent guest, 'You rotate the handle up if you want it to tilt, rotate it down if you want it locked, hold it horizontal and pull if you want the door to slide,' it kept being translated into Agent-speak as, 'Give it a good shouldering if it doesn't do what you want.'

I realised that if a guest couldn't pass the French Door Test (successfully opening both the front door and the balcony widow without assistance) he or she was probably an Agent.

27. THE FRENCH DOOR TEST

Parents are understandably paranoid about crime and insist on having the chalet door locked at all times of the day. Some are worried their kids will be abducted in the middle of the night. The really paranoid will take the key out of the lock and put it somewhere 'safe'. One mother took the key to bed in her dressing-gown pocket - her kids were safe from everything but fire. Unfortunately, other guests were leaving in the morning and were trapped. I frantically searched for the key while their transfer driver waited impatiently outside. They had to pass their suitcases out of a window. They were just about to climb out themselves when I found the key. I'd noticed that parents often turn out to be Agents of Entropy.

Despite my philosophy on crime and possessions, and the extra hassle it creates for me, I now always keep my chalet door locked. The final straw came when I found two Jehovah's Witnesses in the hallway and mistook them for my new guests and tried to show them to their rooms. Ironically, they broke off the encounter, closed the door in my face and beat a hasty retreat.

I'd like to live in a world where doors don't have to be locked and more people knew how to operate French door furniture. However, I now at least have a reliable, and well tested, way of identifying the human Agents of Entropy.

28. The Best Ski Instructor in the World

I was very nervous while waiting for Roland Stieger to arrive at Chalet Framboise. He probably didn't remember me but I certainly remembered him. I don't know why I was nervous; living in Chamonix he probably didn't know I'd written an English book, nor that he was in it, nor that I'd misspelt his name.

The latter mistake could prove useful, I thought; I could pretend I'd been referring to someone else. I thought I'd been reasonably complimentary, in my backhanded way. I'd been afraid of him, I'd admired him, I'd ended up liking him, but I didn't really know him – that was going to change.

Two of my regular guests, Alan and Mark, had asked me to arrange a week's skiing with a 'top' instructor for their exclusive use – the cost wasn't that important. I tried to enlist the services of local instructors who'd taught me, and who I thought where 'top', but none were available for the specified week. I was hesitant to hire someone I'd not skied with myself; it would make a mockery of my recommendation.

I wanted an instructor who would be fun to spend a week with. To my mind, this was more important than their skiing ability. My guests didn't need an elite coach; they were middle-aged piste skiers not powder hounds. They wanted to ski more confidently not downhill race. Although, being competitive in nature, I was worried they wanted to become great skiers overnight or they were looking for a silver bullet to kill all of their ski demons with one shot.

I racked my brains trying to think of someone who would be fun to chat to over lunch but not necessarily, 'the best ski instructor in the world'. Then I recalled those exact words coming out of Roland's mouth two years before. Roland had been a judge on the Ski Club Leaders' course for many years. It was his final thumbs down that had sealed my destiny on my ill-fated first attempt to pass.

28. THE BEST SKI INSTRUCTOR IN THE WORLD

So I found Roland's email address and contacted him with the words, 'You probably don't remember me, but …' I assumed he would be booked up by Arab princes or the French elite who made up his regular client base. To my surprise he was free for the week in question and fancied skiing in Morzine again. Unbeknown to me, it was Morzine where he qualified as an instructor.

I sold Roland to my guests and they agreed to hire him. They were obviously believers in the adage that 'a real expert has to come from at least fifty miles away'. People often think, because they can't find the answer locally, that it must be elsewhere, even if it doesn't exist. We often trust outsiders more than people we know, even if they have the same answers.

Alan and Mark would pay for Roland's accommodation in Framboise, along with his fee. My only remuneration would be to tag along and hopefully get a few skiing tips from the man myself.

That morning my nervous state was exacerbated because, after the deal was done, I realised that I'd never seen Roland teach intermediates. I'd experienced his mentoring off-piste in Tignes, which had been more psychological than practical instruction. In fact, I'd never seen him make an actual ski turn. I was concerned that I'd got the wrong man for the job.

Within the Ski Club, Roland had a reputation for being a Crow Skier - always taking a straight line from A to B at breakneck speed. I'd heard a recent report that the Italian police has arrested him for skiing dangerously fast on one of their pistes. This reinforced my opinion of him and no doubt his opinion of Italians.

In the back of my mind I also knew Roland would be reassessing me again in three years' time when I had to take the Leaders' refresher course. My own skiing would come under his scrutiny and I didn't want him to form any lasting opinions of my ability – especially if they were bad.

He turned up and while he settled in, my angst slowly drained away. I still didn't think he actually remembered failing me, or meeting me at all. I was just another Ski Club Leader and he knew hundreds of them, and we soon both adopted the familiarity of old colleagues. The guests arrived and, being of a similar age and equally debonair, they all hit it off immediately. It was going to be a fun week.

I'm always reluctant to cook for French people, so I took them all to *Le Clin D'Oeil* for dinner. No chap, French or English, wants to attend a dinner party if all of the other diners are blokes. Unfortunately, my Transylvanian fan club were in action plugging my book, and someone from another table came over and asked me to sign a copy. Normally, despite feigning embarrassment, I like the attention so I'm secretly delighted when it happens. It gives existential meaning to my life.

This time the embarrassment was real. I was sitting opposite a man with a real skiing life-story to tell, and compared to his, my own exploits were a joke. Of course, Roland enquired into the contents of the book and worked out that he was probably in it.

I thought this could go one of two ways: either, he'd love my comedy portrait of him and the publicity (which was likely) or be offended and we would all spend the week under an awkward cloud. I made a note to keep the book out of his hands for as long as possible.

Despite the brief interruption when it was embarrassingly all about me, soon the conversation was all about Roland, who entertained us with his stories of life as a guide.

If you wanted to write a biography about a fascinating life in the mountains you'd probably approach Roland. He's spent his life skiing in the winter and climbing in the summer. Previously a member of the Chamonix Gendarmerie rescue team, he was now a private instructor and guide with some impressive and regular clientele. He'd saved many lives and retrieved several dead bodies from crevasses, jumped out of helicopters and dangled in thin air. He'd climbed the North Face of the Eiger, not once but twice, and once chased a bear out of his camp with an ice axe – I would have run in the opposite direction myself.

I learnt that Roland had an English wife, which explained his exceptional command of English and his use of British idioms – it's always amazing to hear them said with a French accent. He said 'bloody hell' with a northern-English accent, leading me to suspect that his wife was a northerner. I hoped he had acquired a northern English sense of humour from her - if he ever read my book he'd need it. I'd previously thought him to be single and a few things I'd written about him might not go down well with his wife, adding to my literary angst.

While listening to his stories, which I knew to be genuine because I'd heard some of them second-hand before, my angst started to well up again. Hiring Roland seemed like overkill for Alan and Mark's requirements – but hell, they'd asked for the best.

After that first dinner, I got the impression they were a little daunted at the prospect of skiing with Roland and so indeed was I - again. He had assured us he would be kind.

Next morning, Roland chose the porridge from my usual English breakfast array – confirming that it is indeed the breakfast of skiing champions. But the weather was not so impressed with our esteemed visitor and we headed up the hill into a dim and damp world with terrible visibility. It hadn't snowed for days and the only snow we could find was second-hand – hard-packed and rutted. Not ideal conditions for teaching nor indeed learning. When you can't see, you always ski more ponderously and your confidence drains away.

After a couple of hours, it was a relief to discover that Roland was good at teaching intermediate piste skiers as well as powder hounds, although he used different terminology and some of his suggestions were contradictory to the BASI doctrine I was more recently used to. I hadn't listened to an ESF instructor for years – unless you count the rant I'd been given through a Land Rover window on the Cresta Run the day the music died.

Alan, who had also more recently had BASI instructors, questioned some of Roland's suggestions. We had a lot of conversations about specifics: width of stance, pole and body position. Alan kept looking for definitive answers when the correct answer to most of the questions was 'it depends on the conditions and the terrain'.

Despite using a different methodology, Roland identified the same faults with my skiing that my BASI trainer (Andy Jerram) had relentlessly been trying to eradicate. The different approach managed to get me a little further past some of my learning difficulties by helping me to approach them in a different way.

A little frustrated with myself, I tried to Ski Like Nobody Was Watching and just do my own thing. This prompted Roland to ask, '*Iz your English so bad, zat you don't understand what I've asked you to do?*' Which was both a sarcastic and humorous thing to say in a second language and partially true. But the language barrier wasn't the problem it was my numerous learning difficulties (now well-documented) that were to blame.

I complained that he only ever seemed to be looking at me when I did a bad turn, which was usually just after I'd done a sequence of beauties. He said, '*Chriz, I'm paid to zee your bad turns, not zee good ones.*' So I decided to ski like nobody was watching and it seemed to work.

Thankfully, lunch was important to Roland, as indeed it is for me. Finding a good restaurant was my job. With no real control of the day's itinerary, I struggled to book a restaurant in advance. We ended up near a tiny restaurant called *Chez Nannon*, which has, in my opinion, the best tartiflette in the Alps. (This is an accolade that is often discussed passionately by chairlift philosophers and is highly subjective).

Unfortunately, it was full of people hiding from the inclement weather. Roland stepped to the rescue; he had a convivial conversation with the *femme de maître d'* in French and before we knew it we were sat in her kitchen drinking wine, our wet gloves hanging over the stove. There was a dustbin full of boiled potatoes in the corner and a glimpse of the tartiflette production line in the adjoining room. Roland chose the wine – he wasn't going to risk leaving that important task to an Englishman.

This wouldn't be the last time a *femme de maître d'* would give me the '*non*' and Roland would then charm out a '*oui*'. The second time, curious to know how he did it, I asked him what he'd said. I thought perhaps I could use the approach myself or at least work out what French etiquette was at play. He'd said he was from Chamonix and had joked he would never return to Morzine unless he could eat in her restaurant tonight. I wasn't sure I could pull that one off.

In between lunch and dinner, the skiing progressed. There were a few eureka moments, when the guys thought they'd 'got it' when something really worked for them, then 'lost it' on the next slope. When learning to ski, you often take one step forward and two steps backwards and so much depends on the condition of the snow and your mental attitude.

There's always a lot of time to talk when skiing. When you're not eating together you're sat side-by-side, on a chairlift. There's a lot of communal waiting around for others too. Over the week we discussed life, wine and philosophy – oh, and occasionally skiing. It seems that living in the company of mountains make philosophers of us all.

I'm not sure if Roland could be classed as an existentialist but his philosophy was kindred to mine. He too didn't seek fortune, although we both agreed being rich would be nice. 'You can't buy my office,' he told me while we were discussing happiness and wealth. He pointed out that he 'could only eat one roast chicken at a time' - and that was all he needed. Now, whenever I'm roasting a chicken, I can't help but think of Roland - I'm hoping this affliction will pass in time.

Towards the end of the week the weather improved and, more importantly, so did the visibility. I thought Roland was making a big difference to the guys' skiing. They seemed to be doing better to my partially trained eyes.

By the time Roland left, I thought the guys had significantly improved and wanted to declare the week a success but Alan was not so sure, perhaps he'd set his aspirations too high. There are no magic bullets in skiing, at least none that I can find. There's no substitute for practise and getting mileage under your skis.

The night before Roland left, I handed him a copy of my book, hoping he'd not get to the part about himself. He jumped straight to the chapter he was in and read out some paragraphs aloud while I twitched. He seemed a bit alarmed at some of the quotes, I'd attributed to him.

I didn't sleep much that night, worrying that I might have offended him. After spending a week getting to know the man, I wished I could replace some of the things I'd written with more accurate words and not simply cast him as a stereotypical crazy French guide.

Now I'm an existentialist, I don't believe in stereotypes and I regret painting him as one. Surprisingly, he bought two copies before departing in the morning, so maybe he liked the portrait I'd painted with my pen more than he let on. Sometimes, a myth can overtake a man, and he has no option but to follow in its path.

29. The Existential Party

It's our parents' fault — everything usually is. They don't give us a choice. They make us attend the party and insist that, with the right attitude, we'll enjoy ourselves. They fail to mention that the party would be full of grownups and other children who've been dragged along. They insist that we play the boring party games — searching for happiness, fame and wealth. They fail to mention, that even if we do enjoy the party, we'll eventually have to leave.

Humans are unique amongst sentient beings in knowing the certainty of their own death. Perhaps it's because we're reasonably good at avoiding it that death plays on our minds. No matter how well we're doing, we can't help wondering what exactly the point is of living at all. To quote (you guessed it) Sartre, 'Life has no meaning the moment you lose the illusion of being eternal.'

Unlike a midlife crisis, you don't have to be old to have an existential one, just old enough to contemplate your own mortality. Which most of us have been doing, on and off, since our parents gave us the bad news - that, inevitably, we're going to die.

Once you're fifteen and know more about life than your parents ever will, you can start your existential journey. You start making your own choices about which parties to attend. However most of us are too busy at the parties, queuing at the buffet or jostling at the bar, to give life much thought until we pass fifty.

When you reach fifty you start to notice that other people have left the party, usually without saying a proper goodbye. I was skiing with an old sheep farmer who summed it up perfectly while we were dangling on a chairlift. He informed me that: 'They're taking them out of our pen now!'

Like all other sentient beings my main objective every day is to avoid injury and disease and to postpone death. My secondary objective is to have some fun and excitement in the process. These objectives are not always compatible, especially if you're taking a long-term view on the first.

My mother initially took care of the primary objective, but now I mostly look after it myself. She now has a self-appointed post on my advisory board, along with the people I love and the friends whose opinions I trust.

I've discovered that when you're an atheist and try to find your own meaning in life you suffer anxiety when it comes to validating that meaning. It's rather absurd committing your life to values and meanings that you invented for yourself – you might as well believe in The Force. You may also end up looking a bit silly if there is a heaven, with a bouncer at the door (God) and, unlike normal bouncers, he does make up the rules; I'm really too much of a skeptic to be an atheist. It might be easier to follow an established faith rather than invent your own. I fancy giving Buddhism a try – I like the way they run their bars and I've already got a bald head.

Just because I don't believe in any of the popular celestial bouncers doesn't make me a nihilist, free to go raping and pillaging and generally doing what I like. My parents installed a moral compass in me and, although the polar variance may occasionally need adjusting, it still basically points north. I know something is moral if I feel good after doing it and I know it's immoral if I feel bad.

29. THE EXISTENTIAL PARTY

I try to listen to those I ride the chairlifts with and see if any of their religions and philosophies might work for me. It's amazing how others live their lives and how they justify them. However, although this makes for useful background research, you can't accept other people's philosophies as valid, you have to find and validate your own yourself. You have to ask yourself three basic questions:

1. 'Why do I exist?'
2. 'Is there any point to life beyond survival?'
3. 'Having got survival nailed, what shall I do next?'

Unlike most existentialists, I'm searching for the answers to those questions on the top of mountains and in the bars at their base - they seem as good a place as any to start. The answers I've come up with so far are: 'I don't know', 'probably not' and 'anything you like' - so long as it doesn't prevent others from doing the same.

After six winters' skiing that's as far as I've got. I'm pretty certain the full answers must be more complicated, or at least I hope they are, otherwise someone or something is having a laugh.

If you're a theist existentialist, and believe in celestial bouncers you've probably got a better set of answers than me, but you'll have several dichotomies to solve first – pain, despair, war and pestilence for starters. You're going to have to answer three ancillary questions too:

4. 'How should I live my life?'
5. 'Where can I go after that?'
6. And, most importantly, 'How do I get in?'

I wish you *bonne chance* with those questions; I'm still working on the first three.

I often look at Oscar with envy, being a dog he has no idea

he is going to die or how much time he has left. He doesn't worry about the future or what other dogs might think. I'm not so envious that he has been spayed and that his life's primary objective, to breed, has been taken away.

Oscar doesn't seem to lose much sleep wondering what the purpose of his life (post nuts) now is. However, he might be struggling with a couple of questions of his own:

7. 'Why did the human overlords chop off my nuts?'
8. 'Why do they covet my poo and collect it in bags?'

If he's a canine philosopher he may well conclude, 'I poo, therefore I am,' and continue his life-long search for biscuits. Of course, he may be an existentialist and decide 'I am, therefore I poo.'

Meanwhile, I need to get the advisory board off my back – they're having none of this meaning-of-life crap. I'll resume my quest for wealth and legacy so I can have a comfortable retirement or be remembered when I'm dead - I might just give the skiing a couple more seasons first.

It could just be that our parents played a prank on us – the same prank our grandparents played on them, by dragging them to a party that wasn't entirely fun. But, you can't live life as if it were a pointless joke - unless you're certain that it is.

Once you're over fifty you lose the assumption that the party will last forever. You also stop assuming that your parents were wrong about everything. Your parents hadn't lied about death either and in some cases, seemingly to prove their point, they left the party themselves. Then you can go looking for meaning in the pointlessness of your life and another existentialist will be born.

30. Keep on Running

The most powerful Agent of Entropy is time. It works away at the human body relentlessly and the effects cannot be undone. Time can't be stopped although its affect can be slowed down. If you look after yourself, you should still be able to ski almost until you die – and preferably on the same day.

At ninety-eight (at the time of writing) George Jedenoff, a powder hound from Utah, is possibly America's oldest living skier. He puts his longevity down to 'not eating too much' and not doing 'anything to excess' – which is sound advice. Scotland's very own Hilda Jamieson has just hung up her skis at the age of 102! Bad eyesight finally made her stop. I guess even for people who regularly ski in Scotland, enthusiasm for skiing with poor visibility wanes.

Assuming the god-of-knees, keeps smiling on me, I anticipate skiing until I die. Obviously, I'll have to stop going off-piste at some stage, mostly because the toilet will be too far way. I probably won't go out in bad weather and I'll avoid using draglifts - so nothing much will actually change. I'm also sure that if I fancy going down the Buddha Bar when I'm eighty, the music will still be the same.

Post fifty, in an attempt to be one of the middle sheep to be taken from my pen, I decided to look after what was left of my health by not eating or drinking so much and I joined the legion of Lycra-wearing middle-aged people who litter our streets.

I've never liked running, but running likes me and it's the only way I know to reliably reduce my waistline. I do like the psychological benefits that running brings. If you have a 'face of wood' it can get rid of 'the cockroach'.

Running helped me defeat the Ski Demons and get my Leader's jacket. If you know you can run for an hour without stopping, you know you can flail around in powder for half an hour, trying to find your skis, without having a heart attack. When it's fit, my body becomes a skiing asset, not a liability waiting to let me down.

Being a 'runner' also means I can join in with those pub conversations that men who wear Lycra at the weekend always seem to have – and not feel guilty about doing so while eating pork scratchings.

Having just returned from Season 5, I found myself having an equally healthy lunch with formerly angry pirate Charlie. He was talking like an athlete while eating a burger. He was obviously having an existential crisis of his own. With his more youthful colleagues, he'd entered a 10K fun run in Sutton Park. I pointed out that the term 'fun run' was an oxymoron but, after downing another couple of pints, he persuaded me to enter too.

Having taken the Hemingway Oath, I trained and trained in an attempt not to be the last person around the park. Then Charlie called me, just before the run, claiming he was injured. None of his colleagues would be running either, all for unspecified reasons.

Even though Charlie's phone call had let me off the Hemingway Hook, I decided to run the race anyway. I finished seventh in the fifty-something category, having overtaken Mr Eighth on the home straight. Mind you he was wearing a T-shirt that said, 'Army Vet – Please Overtake.'

I didn't run much the following summer because I lacked motivation to do so despite being overweight. There were no blue jackets or bragging rights to train for and no skiing courses lined up the next winter for me to potentially fail – and losing weight is always a postponable goal.

30. KEEP ON RUNNING

I didn't get many skiing workouts in Season 6. I girlfriend skied most of the season, which involved a lot of sizable lunches, not aerobic exercise and a net gain in calories per day.

Once you reach your skiing equilibrium and ski only at your comfort level, you seldom burn a significant number of calories. Assuming conditions are good, and the piste is well groomed, skiing blues and the odd red is less aerobic than walking as far as I'm concerned - especially if you stop for *chocolat chaud* half way up and a *vin chaud* half way down.

I was used to returning from the Alps lighter than when I departed - despite eating like a horse and sometimes an actual one. But I came back fat from Season 6.

However, to extend my skiing life I probably needed to keep on the treadmill in the summer and move up the skiing levels in the winter, if my skiing wasn't to go, metaphorically, downhill. I concluded that I was enjoying my skiing too much and needed to set myself some painful skiing goals.

I contemplated taking my BASI Alpine Instructor Level 2. That would involve another thirty-five hours of shadowing,[37] in addition to the painful thirty-five hours I'd already done and then I would have to spend two weeks under a microscope myself. Knowing how much I hated skiing in a Petri dish, it would be a suitably painful, if not impossible, goal.

After that I could take the Level 3 the following season and continue my journey up the BASI skiing hill. I noticed from their website that this would require learning a second language – I wondered if Franglais would count.

I had other age-related issues with the Project in general. I was getting a bit too old for sleeping in a laundry and for driving

---

37 **Shadowing**, in a ski teaching sense, means standing around on the beginner slopes listening to a real instructor and often being a ski-borne nanny for toddlers - it involves very little actual skiing.

drunken people up and down a toboggan run. I was also weary of fighting the Alpine Agents of Entropy. I wondered what was the normal retirement age for a ski bum?

One Monday morning, prior to Season 7, I found myself driving in rush hour around the M42, Birmingham's orbital equivalent to London's M25. Everyone seemed to be late for work and they were giving no quarter to a beaten up old Defender, driven by an even older man in a T-shirt. The human race is always at its worst on a Monday between 8 and 9am, no matter in which city you live. I concluded that a ski bum, however old, could never retire – because he could never go back to this.

A lot of skiers, when they reach a plateau in their alpine skiing, deviate to other disciplines: telemarking, cross-country skiing and, in some radical cases, snowboarding. Perhaps the correct challenge was not in the Alps at all, but closer to home?

I was spending an increasing amount of time fell-walking – rekindling a forgotten passion. Whenever I could get away, I'd head 'Up North'. That summer I met an octogenarian in the Lakes while resting by a tarn. He sat down and started talking to me - I don't think he'd seen another human in a while and I was happy to listen. He soon got on to philosophy; people usually do when surrounded by mountains – the mountains don't have to be covered in snow.

He had completed his Wainwright Challenge[38] for a second time, after having both his hips replaced. Inspired by his endeavour,

---

38 **Alfred Wainwright** MBE (17 January 1907 – 20 January 1991) was a British fell-walker, guidebook author and illustrator. His seven-volume Pictorial Guide to the Lakeland Fells, published between 1955 and 1966, consisted entirely of reproductions of his manuscripts and has become the standard reference work to 214 of the fells of the English Lake District.

30. KEEP ON RUNNING

I wondered if that would do for my final challenge too. I could continue to search for answers on the top of English instead of French, mountains – and enjoy significantly better beer in between.

I was starting to realise that I'd been very lucky in the geo-lottery that is the place of our birth - the north of England has some satisfying views, they aren't exclusively the preserve of the Alps.

I started running again, if only for running's sake. I wouldn't enter any more races, I'd literally got the T-shirt for that, but it might buy me some time and keep the weight off. I might retire from skiing one day but if I didn't replace it with another never-ending challenge, I'd have no reason to get out of bed.

31. Vallée de la Manche

It was April and Season 6 was almost over. I hadn't done much skiing in Morzine and none off-piste with Val and David (a.k.a. The Ski Nazis). The snow hadn't been very good that season; it had turned up late and not hung around. However, that wasn't the main reason I'd not done much skiing. I'd been preoccupied with breaking in the new chalet (Framboise), selling books and fighting the Agents of Entropy.

Val & David had spent most of their visits to Morzine with less able friends and were a little tired of Girlfriend Skiing. I'd been invited along on a few occasions, but what friends often don't grasp is that I'm not on holiday even if it looks like I am, and I can't often get away.

Many of my good friends visit Morzine and stay elsewhere. I'm keen to see them on and off the piste but my paying guests are often inconsiderate and make their own plans for me. In frustration, like a true prima donna, I sometimes find myself saying, 'If you want to ski with me, you need to stay with me.'

Since getting my blue jacket, I hadn't led the Ski Nazis anywhere. Being big fans of the Club, they had encouraged me to become a Leader and were delighted, if a little surprised, when I managed to become one – almost as surprised as myself. They would have made great leaders themselves. In fact, David had effectively been my leader for decades.

The opportunity finally presented itself. I had no guests and they were in town and we arranged to go skiing. Not being on official business, I wouldn't be wearing blue but I'd agreed to take them for an off-piste adventure.

Knowing they knew the PdS inside and out too, I was racking my brains for a suitably impressive itinerary and one they hadn't done before when I settled on the *Vallée de la Manche* (VDLM).

The VDLM is Morzine's most beautiful backcountry area. In a world of amazing mountain views it's hard for one to stand out, but the view down the VDLM does just that. It has everything – except possibly wildebeest. In the winter, I'm spoilt and often forget that the purpose of skiing (and of my new life) is to look up as well as down.

Although, in the right conditions, the VDLM is not especially difficult to ski, it's a very extensive area and it's hard to navigate and, being south-facing, it's avalanche prone. So it's not an area you'd go into without a local guide or someone who's successfully been down it before.

Framboise is at the bottom of the valley and it's theoretically possible, given enough snow, to ski back to the chalet using a path on the other side of the river. I'd spent a lot of time that season walking up the path with Debbie to the romantically named *Lac des Mines d'Or* (the Gold Mine lake), which was at its top. It's a delightful and easy walk that made her feel she was up in the high Alps without donning the dreaded skis. It also made me wonder why I bother with the planks too.

The road winds through pine trees up to the lake and is tranquil – until some cross-country skiers come careering round the corner, politely screaming '*Excusez-moi,*' or their equivalent in Franglais. Pine forests are very noise absorbent. On a still day, there's often only the tweet of birds and your own breathing to be heard. Often, when skiing down forest paths the noise from your skis prevents you enjoying the forest tranquillity so I often stop, let everyone go ahead and listen to the silence – then I nip behind a tree and have a pee.

Above the lake the proper skiing starts on the slopes of the connecting valleys, with not a piste in sight. The valleys funnel down to the lake from three directions. To access them, you take the *Fornet* lift from Avoriaz to the top of the *Fornet* peak (2,250m) and then hike up to the *Col de Fornet*, 100m to its right. It's only 100m of ascent from the chair, using foot holes created by those who have gone before. I'm not one for massive hikes in ski boots.

Two days before our expedition, I'd been up to the lake with Debbie. While basking in the sun, the tranquillity had been interrupted by a loud rumbling noise. Even if you've never seen or heard an avalanche you'll know what the noise means and look up with dread.

We were in no danger. The lake's collection of old mine huts had stood for decades and we were a long way from any significantly snow-covered slope. We looked up and saw the avalanche in action on the side of the valley: great big chunks of ice tumbling down the valley flashing their brown bottoms that had previously been sat on the earth, leaving a bare patch of soil behind. With my binoculars I could see some ski tracks above the patch and hoped they were several days old.

March avalanches are possibly the worse to get caught in. Warm daytime temperatures melt the snow, which freezes again overnight. The snow becomes very hard packed and when it finally loses its grip on the mountain, it comes tumbling down in large chunks. They usually happen in the afternoon after one last heating session from the sun. In spring, you want to ski late enough in the day for the snow to have softened and be pleasant to ski on, but not so late that it slides down the mountain with you. Being thrown into a cement mixer with a load of rocks and ice means you'll probably get pummelled to death rather than the usual fate in a powder avalanche: suffocating to death. There's no way to ski out of an ice avalanche either – it would be like skiing across boulders of stone.

I met Val and David at a cafe in Avoriaz at around 10am. We had a 'Spring Snow' debate. There's always a debate, if only in the guide's head, as to the safety of the intended route. Was it best to wait for the sun to do some more of its softening work or risking being in a south-facing valley too late in the day? We had another coffee then set off.

I was particularly nervous. Val & David had left the final decision to me and I was more worried, after seeing the avalanche the previous day, that this had become a foolhardy mission. The more you learn about mountain safety the more you see the anatomy of a disaster in every situation. But then the safest thing is to never get out of bed.

I happily trust real guides that I hardly know with such decision making, their only credentials being that they're old and still alive, but I don't seem to trust myself. I was worried that the opportunity for us to ski together had presented itself and that my desire to do something exciting with my old friends was clouding my judgement.

We got off the *Fornet* chair and did our transceiver checks and then started the climb. We met a snowboarder climbing down which wasn't a good sign. He told us that the snow was still too crusty for him and he was going to wait a bit longer. I dismissed this because boarding is even more unpleasant in icy conditions than skiing.

The feeling of impending doom was lifted when we found an ESF guide at the top with his client, about to descend. I don't know why this was so reassuring. I tend to think of the ESF as invincible. However, only the day before I'd been stuck in a traffic jam caused by the funeral cortège of an ESF guide, killed in an avalanche on the *Col De Cou* – the adjacent valley.

It had been a bad season for mountain accidents in the PdS. Sometimes the snowpack builds up and behaves unpredictably when the weather is freakish. A warm January never creates a good base. On two occasions avalanches had made it onto the pistes in Morzine – something you never used to expect. There'd been several warnings, including one from the Ski Club safety officer, that the snow pack was especially unstable that season.

After exchanging pleasantries with the guide and concluding that not all ESF folk are the same, we asked his advice. He concluded, '*iz never completely safe in zee mountains,*' and gave us the sign that he was a true mountain philosopher by executing a perfect Gallic shrug.

He walked off further up the left side of the Col, his charge looking a bit miffed that his climb wasn't over. Not wanting to be cheeky and follow him without paying, I headed straight down with mine.

We soon discovered that the snow, if you could call it that, had not been over exposed to the sun and was safe. The bad news was that it was almost un-skiable - covered in ruts and frozen tracks. We (or I) had committed us to a couple of hours of teeth-chattering descent. It didn't help that we were all wearing wide powder skis - in my case out of optimism and in theirs through lack of choice. We always tend to select our skis for the conditions we want to ski in, not the ones we're most likely to find.

At least we could admire the views during our frequent stops while I tried to choose the optimal route forward. On a previous descent, I'd gone too low and ended up skiing off a small cliff and having to climb back up it.

Half way down I took us hard to the left to avoid repeating the mistake and ended up at the top of the debris from the avalanche I'd seen while walking with Debbie the day before. The good news was that avalanches don't fall twice; the bad news was that we were wearing skis not crampons and turning between the lumps of solid ice proved almost impossible. At one stage, I attempted to jump off one boulder, rotate 180 degrees and land on the next – a manoeuvre that was only partly successful but got a round of applause.

Slightly winded, I started to panic and the Ski Demons, long since silenced, started to chirp up in my head. My fellow ice warriors seemed to be doing better, although you never know what demons are talking in other people's heads.

Finally, defeated, I took off my skis and crawled to the edge of the debris. I sat there hyperventilating and realised I was sitting far too close to a cornice. Realising the peril I might be in I tried to remount my skis. However, it was too steep and the snow wasn't soft enough for me to fashion a mounting platform. David tried to help me, as he'd done for so many years – the master once again had become the student. I slid down on my bum to a flat bit, something a guide seldom does.

I skied behind David like a beginner, until we regrouped further down the valley. I noticed a flock of passerine birds fly past. They were too far away to identify their species, but to see a flock of perching birds meant either summer or the treeline were not too far away.

The drama was mostly in my head but it reminded me that the most important part of being a good skier off-piste is staying cool and never, ever, taking your skis off until you're on the flat. Had I not been with them maybe I'd have kept it more together. Maybe I shouldn't have gone first, maybe I should have followed the ESF guide – maybe I shouldn't have been in the VDLM in late March?

Finally, we arrived at the old gold mine and were out of any danger. We skied down the road ruining the tranquillity of those walking up it and flopped on to a table outside *La Crapahute* (some names really don't pronounce well in Franglais). I'm not sure who gave the restaurant its name. The proprietor, Mark, a cheeky and mischievous expat, brought us a bottle of rosé which must have been leaking and soon had to be replaced. He makes the best goat's cheese omelette in the Alps and possibly the world – so we ordered three.

We sat in the sun, laughing and joking about how awful the skiing had been, with sweat and bits of cheese drying on our faces. The wine could have been warm and the omelette rank but food always tastes better when you feel that you've earned it and it was the best lunch we'd had in a while. It might not have been the best day's skiing either and I had not proved to be the best of ski guides, but it felt like old times.

The best way to return from Mark's inebriated is on a toboggan. I've done this from other low mountain restaurants and it proves exceptionally entertaining and deceptively hazardous given the competitive nature of most pissed blokes. Once in *Megève*, coming down on toboggans after a rather boozy dinner, we lost someone. Due to a lack of command structure and torches, our search proved ineffective. We finally found the individual ineffectually climbing out of a stream just to the left of the road, toboggan on his head. He claimed that an unidentified villain had forced him off the road – I suspect it might have been me.

Fortunately, we had skis, not toboggans, so we skied part way back down the path to the chalet, until the snow became too watery for gravitation to propel us through it, then we jumped on a bus. Tired, battered and relieved, after a first descent of the VDLM for them and an educational one for me, we were all full of post-adventure euphoria and all very much still alive. I now know that you can never completely kill your ski demons, they're always lurking somewhere in the back of your head.

32. Midlife Clarity

Season 7 was afoot. The clocks had gone back and British Summer Time was officially over. It was time to forget existentialism and return to hedonism, Chalet Framboise and the Alps. I would be returning to a more dangerous environment with better views.

The housework was all done, if not the cooking, but I was going back to more discerning diners and more appreciative guests. My first-world problems could be put on ice (snow) for another winter and my insomnia would be cured by exhaustion.

Instead of being the best supporting actor in a doctor's life, I'd once again be playing the lead in my own – although Debbie's play was a life-and-death drama and mine was more of a situation comedy. It was time for me to rejoin the caste of formerly Angry Pirates, BASI Ballerinas, Saga Louts, Cougars and Soggy Bottom Boys. What devious tricks would the Agents of Entropy play on me – and how would they materialise?

Would Landie make it to the Alps for a seventh consecutive time and would we both keep our grip on the now infamous Cresta Run? Would my return to Laax, as Vanessa, be a success? Was this the season I'd finally master short turns in powder and would Debbie conquer her Ski Demons allowing us to ski together - à *deux*?

Was I truly over the Ardent Incident and had existentialism actually helped? Would I ever get a respectable summer job and rejoin the human race? Would I ever leave the Witness-Protection programme and find a summer view worthy of a gaze? Would I finally master French conjugation and say '*adieu*' to Franglais?

I had a lot of unanswered questions. However, sometimes certainty is more stressful than the unknown. Certainty removes hope from life's equation and it's best if the future isn't entirely known. It's the certainty and finality of death that causes existential angst.

I know wanting to look only at beauty is an unrealistic ambition. To truly appreciate a good view you need to look on ugliness first. Spending another winter going up, only to come down might seem pointless. But as all chairlift philosophers know - the journey is more important than the destination. I also know it's unrealistic for a dyslexic to learn a second language before he's mastered his first.

However I have accidentally used over a hundred French words, pretending to be English ones, in this book. So maybe an old ski dog *can* learn new tricks and one day he will be able to ski successfully through the trees. I've pretty much accepted that I'll never be in a Miller movie or be asked to play James Bond, but my skiing equilibrium could just be one more level up.

Becoming an existentialist (whatever that means) had provided me with more than just excuses. When you *exist* without a permanent home, have no children nor a God, having freewill can seem like a curse. How do you make responsible and rational decisions in an irrational and irresponsible universe? The only way to find meaning in life is to embrace existence. There is no right or wrong way to live your life, as long as no innocent bystanders get hurt.

But I've had enough of worrying about the future and the past - it's taken enough fun out of existing, lost me enough sleep and created too much angst. This season I'm going to ski like nobody is watching and worry about all that unimportant stuff when I get back. However before I go I need to print some T-shirts that say - 'I am, therefore I ski'.

Bloody Book II is now finished and Debbie hopes it will be my last. I now have two offspring of my own (SWD-I & SWD-II) and maybe that's enough. Debbie, like a bemused stepparent, is wondering why I spent so much time and effort bringing them to life. But they've partially satiated my need for legacy and, better still, I haven't had to drag them to the existential party or put them through school.

And if you're wondering what happened to *Le Chat Noir*, I have a final update. The cleaner paid for her to stay at the vets where her litter was delivered. Then a guest, obviously a feline fanatic, took her home to England. Turns out that black cats are actually very lucky after all.

Even though I know the war cannot be won, I'll continue to fight the Agents of Entropy and savour the battles that I do win - I accept that there'll always be chaos and disorder in my life, when other people are around. 'Hell is other people', Sartre might be right, but I need lots of other people to make my skiing world go round.

FINISH